The HOUSE *at*
"ROCKY ACRES"
&
Other True Tales

The HOUSE at "ROCKY ACRES" & Other True Tales

BY

ANNA MARIA MALKOÇ

To Cousin Brian & Margaret Jones
and Family, in faraway UK,
with love, Cousin Anna Maria Malkoç,
Edmonds, Washington, USA, Jan. 2012

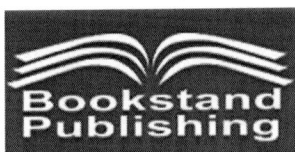

Bookstand Publishing

www.bookstandpublishing.com

Published by
Bookstand Publishing
Morgan Hill, CA 95037
3315_5

ISBN 978-1-58909-898-5

Printed in the United States of America

Cover design and color restorations by Ron Carraher
About the Author photograph by Hikmet Lillian Malkoç

DEDICATION *to* MY GRANDSONS

This collection of **"True Tales"** is dedicated to the main figures in the last five stories — my three grandsons:

Gordon Malkoç Loop *son of my third daughter Melike Malkoç* whose names honor his Turkish grandfather Selahattin Malkoç and his American grandfather Brooks Loop;

Dylan Sharief Malkoç *son of my only son Timur* whose names honor his Iraqi grandfather Ahmat Sharief and his Turkish grandfather Selahattin Malkoç; and

Miles Jonathan Malkoç *son of my only son Timur* whose names honor his American grandfather Jonathan Fields and his Turkish grandfather Selahattin Malkoç.

May these young boys grow to become worthy citizens, honoring their ancestors and family, and respecting life on this planet.

Grandmother **Anna Maria Malkoç**

APPRECIATION *to* MY MOTHER

It was my mother, Marie Harms Jones, who encouraged me to start a written correspondence with my cousin Lucile on her father's wheat farm, 70 miles west of my hometown of Spokane WA. That summer I was nearly eight, old enough to print a short message on a penny postcard and mail it. In 1933, it was a real thrill to exchange penny postcards every week with my cousin.

In 1938, it was another thrill to learn about "Pen Pals," a new organization for American school children. Then, when I learned that it cost *"only a dime"* to receive the address of a Pen Pal in a foreign country, I despaired, never having *owned* a dime. It was still the Great Depression, and my parents had to count every penny. Somehow, however, after my mother read the Pen Pal announcement, she unearthed a dime to put in the mailing envelope, and a three-cent stamp to mail it.

Eventually, my teacher received the name and address of a Pen Pal for me and I wrote him a letter. In response, I received such an amazing letter from such a different world that I couldn't believe my eyes. I read and re-read it, put it away in my treasure box, then put it out of my mind. I was going on 14 years old at the time. *[See Story 18, My Exotic Pen Pal,* and the three up-to-date *Epilogues.]*

During the seventy some years of my life that followed, World War Two began and ended, I entered and finished college, married a fellow student, and went off to spend a decade with him in his exotic country. When my mother mentioned me once to her newspaper-editor friend in Spokane, he requested a story about my "interesting life" for his Sunday paper. At that time, we were living near the ancient Tigris River in a remote oil camp encircled by oil rigs and derricks.

I struggled to type out an article for the editor on my portable typewriter, and mailed it from the tiny post office near a Kurdish area close to the end of the Turkish railroad line.

The editor's response was to send me a printed copy in his Sunday newspaper — in which, I noticed, *he had not changed one word.* This was so encouraging, I was inspired to write more articles, and after my second retirement, to self-publish my autobiography and some short stories for my family. Looking back now, I realize my life-long passion for writing really began with printing messages on penny postcards. For this inspiration, I owe thanks to my mother. ***The Author***

ACKNOWLEDGEMENTS

Special thanks go to my brother **John Harms Jones** of Spokane, Washington, first of all, for discovering the twenty-acre plot of land for sale that became the "Rocky Acres" of this story. Thanks also to John for sharing a wealth of details about his seven decades of life in the region. His interesting details have immeasurably enhanced this key story: *The House at "Rocky Acres."*

It is also fortunate to have sharp-eyed, perceptive friends who are willing to read my rough drafts, and to comment on such things as general interest, vocabulary, and clarity; I take every comment to heart. Along the way, they pick up on typos and other errors I've overlooked, an invaluable help to any writer:

Maggie Dale, instructor at the Japanese Women's College, Mukogawa Fort Wright Institute in Spokane WA. In addition to draft reading, **Maggie** also helped me in the selection of the key story, *The House at "Rocky Acres,"* out of the 18 stories in this collection.

Mary Hovander, retired nurse and neighbor in Edmonds WA, has faithfully read (in draft) every page of the last three E-books I've written in Edmonds.

Gudrun Middell, former instructor at Leipzig U, now translator in Leipzig, Germany, considers reading my drafts a "linguistic challenge." In answering her thoughtful questions about the drafts, I always learn something new and interesting about language.

Courtney Lee, student/computer graphics consultant and her mother, formatter **Leslie Lee** in Mukilteo WA, helped me out with some intricate computer processes.

Ron Carraher, cover designer, has patience and an artistic eye in interpreting the author's wishes. He truly distinguishes whatever he touches.

Finally, I must thank my immediate family: daughters **Kâmuran Shanti Malkoç** in Aberdeen, **Melike Eden Malkoç** in Seattle, and son **Timur Malkoc** in Mukilteo, for encouraging me throughout this book project; and I especially thank my first daughter, **Hikmet Lillian Malkoç** in Edmonds, for being my live-in technical consultant. Without her patient guidance and dedicated encouragement, I would never have been able to format and complete this collection of memoirs.

The Author

TABLE *of* CONTENTS

APPENDIX: STORY NOTES

1

MY BRAVE GRANDMOTHER
Homesteading on the Prairie, circa 1890

PROLOGUE *Before I begin, I must explain a word in the title of this story: "brave." I do not consider my daughter Kâmuran's grandmother (my mother Marie — the heroine of this little story) the only brave one in my family. After listening to family stories about childhood days, I regard all my ancestors as brave. Life was hard for everyone in those days; not every child even survived infancy.*

When my daughter Kâmuran was in the fourth grade at Janney Elementary School in Washington DC, she asked me to tell her a story about her ancestors. This was an assignment for her writing class, she explained: the students were to print parts of the story on separate pages, and the teacher would help them "publish" the pages into their own "books."

I gave some thought to Kâmuran's request, finally remembering a short anecdote my mother had told me from her childhood. I suggested Kâmuran entitle it: "My Brave Grandmother."

Kâmuran's carefully printed-out composition was on exhibit in her classroom for many weeks, but it never survived all our traveling as we moved from country to country for my teaching assignments. So, what follows here now is an attempt to recapture the gist and spirit of Kâmuran's simple story.

My Grandmother Marie grew up in a large family. At the time of this story, there were nine children born in the family, mostly girls. My aunts were Edna, Camilla, Suzanne, Anna, Bertha, Elsie (who died in infancy), and Lillian. My uncles were Walter and Harris.

They all lived on a "homestead" in central Washington State in the late 1800s. In those days, houses out in the countryside were built simply, with no electricity or indoor plumbing, no running water, bathtub, or toilet.

Instead, each house had a well nearby, where the family pumped water and carried it into the house, and an outdoor toilet called an "outhouse." This was a deep pit dug into the ground farther from the house, with a wooden seat built over it, and a wooden shed built over the seat.

My grandmother's sister Anna (sometimes called Ann, or Annie) was two years older than my grandmother Marie, but she was a timid child, afraid of many things. Marie always helped her, especially at night when they had to walk down the path to the outhouse.

Excerpts from the Eggert Harms family photo, Wilbur, WA. c 1900

Marie Agnes Harms
Age 6 (born in 1894)

Anna Eleanor Harms
Age 8 *(born in 1892)*

The younger children weren't afraid if they had to go down the path during the day or on moonlight nights, because then the moon shone as bright as daylight.

But on nights with no moon, however, everything was pitch-black, and the children were "scaredy cats." They held hands all the way down the path and back.

On the dark, moonless night of this story, Marie and her sister Anna were walking hand-in-hand together along the path. Suddenly, Anna screamed: "Oh, Marie! Help! Is that a snake?" She pointed to a dark shape on the path. The children had been warned over and over again about the snakes, especially rattlesnakes, in the region. They were deadly poisonous.

"Where? Where?" Marie shouted, instinctively picking up a piece of an old fence post that had fallen near the path. She tiptoed to where her sister was pointing. In the darkness, she could barely see the long, thin shape curled on the path. Moving quickly before the snake could strike, she began to beat it with all her strength. Finally, she was exhausted and had to stop to rest.

She watched the shadows carefully. When she was sure nothing was moving, she said, "It's OK now, Annie. Let's go!" Carrying the stick in one hand, and her sister's hand in the other, they returned to the big farmhouse. She decided to keep the stick. It was a useful weapon.

The next day, Marie went out to look at the enemy she had beaten to death in the dark. There it was, lying motionless in their path. In the bright light of the morning sun, she could now see it clearly. To her surprise, she saw that it was simply a long, long coil of dark brown rope.

EPILOGUE *My daughter Kâmuran's story of her Grandmother Marie's courage in the face of perceived danger serves as a reminder today that often not only children, but grown-up adults as well, may become paralyzed with fear. Then they are unable to act or think logically, to consider options or possible solutions to their problems.*

Simply shedding a little light on a difficult situation sometimes helps clear it up.

2

LIFE *on a* WHEAT FARM
Wilbur, Washington   c 1930s

PROLOGUE *My hardworking mother was usually too tied down with housework to travel long distances, but she always seized an opportunity to take us children on short trips.*

One of the earliest recollections I have, around the age of two or three, is of Papa driving us all in the old Model T Ford sedan to the small town of Wilbur, some 70 miles west of Spokane in Washington State. We were on our way to visit Mama's parents — our German grandfather and grandmother, whom we all called Grossvater and Grossmutter.

Shortly after we arrived at our grandparents' house with the big kitchen, the grown-ups came back from attending the German Lutheran church service just up the street. Soon, there was a great Sunday dinner steaming on the long dining table: large dishes of mashed potatoes and gravy, fried chicken, green peas and diced carrots, with apple pie for desert. Many years later, I realized that all the food came from Grossmutter's garden and chicken house, and my aunts had cooked the delicious dinner.

I remember Grossvater sitting silently at the head of the table that day, and Grossmutter smiling and chatting away at the other end.

My Uncle Elsworth Brock and Aunt Ann were there with their daughter Lucile, visiting from their nearby farm.

Papa, Mama, my brothers David and John sat near us while baby brother Aaron lay sleeping in a basket in the corner of the dining room. Like us, Uncle Jack the barber, Aunt Suzanne, and Cousin Donald, had driven from Spokane that Sunday.

As I sat high up in the spindly wooden highchair, it seemed like a very large group of grown-ups, all eating and talking and laughing. After dinner, I was taken outside to play with my cousin Lucile, a year older than myself.

This exciting outing was the first clear memory I have of my Wilbur relatives, who became an important part of my early life.

M y very first solo visit to Cousin Lucile on the Brock farm was the summer when I was old enough to read road signs, and could be trusted to follow directions. I must have been around eight.

Growing up as an only child, Lucile was excited to have a real playmate come to visit her on the farm. She first took me to see how she gathered eggs from the chicken coop, and explained that this was her regular chore. Then she showed off the new brown-and-white calf in the barn, and the litter of tiny calico kittens down by the willows. All the calves and cats had interesting names, as if they were her playmates, I noticed.

Note 1. Cousin Lucile and her Half-brother Merle. See Appendix

Lucile's father, my Uncle Elsworth, was a farmer transplanted from "Ioway." He was of Pennsylvania Dutch extraction, Lucile told me in a proud little tone of voice. At the time, I had no idea where "Ioway" was. I knew that my grandparents were from the "Old Country" in Germany, but I didn't know that Pennsylvania Dutch simply meant Germans who lived in Pennsylvania. Nine-year-old Lucile seemed to know so much about geography and farms — and the world. Mama was right, I thought. You do learn a lot when you travel!

Uncle Elsworth was a quiet man of few words. When Lucile reminisced about him years later, I found it hard to believe that before he married Aunt Ann, he used to play the fiddle for the Saturday night Grange dances on nearby Sherman Road.

I remember Uncle Elsworth as a tall, handsome man, wrestling 16 to 20 workhorses into their harnesses and driving them to the wheat fields to work. He always took good care of his animals because he depended on them: it took all of them to pull the plow or the seeder in the spring, and the huge threshing machine at harvest time in the late summer. During harvest, he had to hire a crew to help out. Even as a small child, I could see this was all very hard work.

Aunt Ann, I could see, worked equally hard. To get all the water for their daily needs, she had to hand-pump it from the well into galvanized buckets, then carry the heavy water buckets down the path into the house for drinking, cooking, washing hands, washing dishes, washing clothes, house cleaning, and taking Saturday night baths.

Every morning, Aunt Ann cleaned out the cook-stove and carried out the ashes, then carried in firewood to start a fresh fire for the day. The cast-iron cook-stove not only heated the huge kitchen, it heated the oven for baking, and the surface plates of the stove for cooking, steaming, boiling, and simmering food. In the reservoir on the side of the huge stove, it heated all the water needed for washing dishes three times every day.

Although it wasn't apparent to me until I was an older child, one of Aunt Ann's household chores was also carrying out several large china chamber pots -- one for each bedroom -- to empty in the outhouse each morning. She would rinse each pot first with soapy water and then fresh well water, and empty the water around the roots of a scraggly little pine tree near the gate. The poor, stunted tree also received regular dousings of used dishpan water three times a day, but in that bleached, acidic soil, it never really thrived at all.

Morning and evening, regularly, Uncle Elsworth milked the six cows in the barn before going about his other chores, and Aunt Ann carried the buckets of warm milk into the cooling house and poured it into large flat pans to cool so she could separate off the cream. Later, she would churn the cream into butter; she saved the resulting buttermilk for drinking and cooking.

In addition, she raised chickens and turkeys and sold their eggs, along with the fresh butter she churned. Every Saturday morning, Uncle Elsworth drove into Wilbur to shop at Hankels' Dry Goods Store & General Merchandise, where regular customers came in to buy kitchen staples and household sundries as well as fresh farm produce on Saturdays. Aunt Ann had many regular customers for her chickens, butter and eggs.

As there was no electricity on the farm, she did all of the housework by hand: sweeping, washing, scrubbing, and cleaning. She ironed with flatirons heated at the back of the cast-iron kitchen stove. During harvest time, she had the additional responsibility of preparing three nourishing meals a day for the hired men as well: food that would "stick to their ribs."

Even as a child, her jobs, I could see, were just as hard for her as Uncle Elsworth's work was for him, but I cannot recall either Aunt Ann or Uncle Elsworth ever complaining about the drudgery of their daily chores. Whenever quiet Uncle Elsworth *did* make a comment, it was usually brief, with a dry wit, while Aunt Ann always had a commonsensical and humorous comment to make about "life's ups and downs."

Every day except Saturdays and Sundays, if her early morning chores were finished in time before lunch, Aunt Ann would turn on the radio and listen to the 15-minute soap opera, *One Man's* Family (one of the earliest soap operas). This beloved serial opened and closed with romantic strains of sweetly nostalgic organ music, while an announcer advertised the virtues of Rinso soap powder. As a loyal fan, Aunt Ann used Rinso on Monday washdays. "You could always tell it was washday a mile away from the Rinso fragrance in the air."

By the time Lucile and I were in our early teens, she had learned to do a lot of the kitchen work to help her mother. During my visits, I only learned to dry the dishes and set the table, but together we had the daily chore of rounding up the cows from the pasture and herding them into the barn in the late afternoons. After supper, and after all the evening milking chores were done, Uncle Elsworth and Cousin Q, the hired hand, would sit in their rocking chairs in the parlor and read by the bright glow of the Luxor lamp. From time to time, someone would look up and share a bit of interesting information from *The Wilbur Register*, *The Farmer's Almanac*, or the latest ads in the *Sears & Roebuck* and *Montgomery Ward* catalogues.

Sometimes they would work on a group jigsaw puzzle, or challenge Lucile to a board game of Parcheesi or Chinese checkers, or a card game called "Fish."

Aunt Ann's reading tastes were more romantic: she doted on the popular Zane Grey novels about life in the Old West. Like her daily soap opera, the novels added a romantic touch to her isolated world on the ranch. In the glass-fronted bookcase in the parlor, she kept a private stash of Zane Grey novels to read in the evenings. Lucile and I, already avid readers, devoured them in her bedroom upstairs.

My all-time favorite was *Riders of the Purple Sage*. This was manna for my imagination! I would picture Lucile and me in cowgirl outfits, tethering our faithful old horses to a clump of sage brush, making a campfire to heat up the coffee pot, baking potatoes in the hot coals, and then, when sleep overtook us after an adventurous day, spreading our blankets on the ground and sleeping a dreamless sleep under the glittering stars.

Although I always thought of Lucile as an only child, she used to have a half-brother named Merle. *See: Lucile's Half-Brother Merle in Appendix.*

Lucile was always excited to have a real playmate come to visit her on the farm. She always first took me to see how she gathered eggs from the chicken coop, and explained that this was her regular chore. Then she showed off the new brown-and-white calf in the barn, and the litter of tiny calico kittens down by the willows. All the calves and cats had interesting names, like they were her playmates, I noticed.

The closest that Lucile and I ever came to an actual cowgirl life was not riding side-saddle atop one of Uncle Elsworth's enormous plow horses (which gave you a red rash, or saddle sores, if you rode it bareback). Rather, it was singing to the brown-and-white spotted cows as we herded them into the barn each evening, our daily chore. We would switch them ahead of us with slender willow branches, to keep them from wandering away as we trudged over the bumpy terrain. All the while, we would be singing endless verses of our favorite songs: *Red River Valley, Annie Laurie, In the Gloaming,* and *Home on the Range.* Way out in the pasture, we two girls could sing at the top of our voices; no one would hear us except the cows.

"And they don't care," as Cousin Lucile loved to remark.

Aunt Ann & Uncle Elsworth Brock

*Happy retirees, after years of tending to their
plow horses, milk cows, chickens, and acres of wheat fields.*

EPILOGUE *My experiences on the Brock farm in the 1930s enriched my early life in so many ways. Like numerous things in life, I came to appreciate this more as I grew older. My summer visits to the farm gave me special perspectives on what life was like in the "olden days," before the REA (Rural Electrification Association) set up electric power lines along Sherman Road. That was around the time of World War II.*

Ironically, just when Aunt Ann could finally enjoy the convenience of electricity, running water and indoor plumbing in the old wooden farmhouse, Uncle Elsworth felt his bones getting old and "creaky," and declared it was time for him to retire. The couple moved to a little bungalow in Spokane Valley next door to Elsworth's brother, Orville Brock. Now in their cozy house, an oil furnace in the basement conveniently warmed them in the winter, and an air conditioner magically cooled them in the summer.

For Aunt Ann, diligent farmwife for fifty-some years, having a wealth of modern conveniences — hot and cold running water, indoor plumbing, and the marvels of an electric refrigerator, kitchen range, toaster, electric percolator, vacuum cleaner, washing machine, and steam iron — altogether transformed her into the Modern Housewife of her dreams. Nearby supermarkets provided all the food she needed to buy. Then, marvel of marvels, television brought the whole modern world right into their home.

Aunt Ann now had time to rest, and to visit her neighbors. On a regular basis, for an even more exciting outing, one of my older brothers would take Aunt Ann and our mother Marie to explore antique shops on a Saturday afternoon. The two sisters would finish off the afternoon by going to a local drugstore soda fountain for their favorite treat: a root-beer float and a scoop of vanilla on top, with two straws. Giggling like teen-agers, they declared this drugstore treat was "heavenly!"

As for Uncle Elsworth, one of the first things he did in retirement was to set up an electric sprinkler system around the house that kept his lawn emerald green, and the flowerbeds abloom in season.

His pride and joy, though, was the new electric jigsaw in the garage, where he made wooden lawn furniture from "Popular Mechanics" magazine patterns, and clever wooden rocking chairs and stools for his grandchildren. These he painted in charming, bright colors and they became cherished family keepsakes.

So, like his fiddling for the Grange dances of long ago, the dramatic change in Uncle Elsworth's environment brought out another artistic, creative side to this stalwart, mild-mannered tiller of the soil.

May these two dear souls rest in Eternal Peace.

3

The HOUSE *at* " ROCKY ACRES"
Spokane, Washington 1940

PROLOGUE *When our cozy house on South Perry Street in Spokane had to be sold during the Great Depression of the 1930s, we moved into an old row house on Third Avenue. The rent was cheap, and the location was conveniently close to Papa's radiator repair garage, just around the corner on Second Avenue.*

Some six years later, however, the house had become far too small for our growing family. Unbenownst to us younger children, our parents had been discussing whether to move to a frame house on 4th Avenue, or perhaps someplace west of Spokane, in the Gardens Springs area.

At the same time, the owner of the rental house gave Papa the option of buying the old house, or vacating it within two months: he wanted to raze the property and sell it to a downtown car dealer for a new car lot.

It was the first day of summer vacation in 1940 when my second brother, John Harms Jones, pedaled westward on his bike, out past the city limits of Spokane and up the five-mile-long Sunset Highway grade. He was earnestly bound on an inspired mission: to look at the plats he'd been told were listed for sale on Rural Route 4, somewhere west of town above Indian Canyon.
Note 1. Indian Canyon and Local Roads: see Appendix.
Note 2. The Local Spokane Tribe: see Appendix.

John Explores the Area for a Suitable Building Site
It was easy for brother John to spot the small *Rural Route 4* signpost near the top of the Sunset Highway grade. He turned off the highway onto a narrow dirt road curving down into a quiet hollow.

Slowly, he pedaled along to get a good look at a small unpainted, two-room house and its cluster of outbuildings sprawled next to the road in the hollow. These ramshackle buildings, and the mailbox nailed to a fence-post, were the first signs of habitation.

The road continued on upward from the hollow on a curving incline, and leveled out around the next bend. Several large signs posted near the edge of the road immediately caught his eye: ***Private Property - No Trespassing*** and ***LOTS for SALE,*** with a surveyor's map of numbered plats. He noted the size of the plats and their proximity to the highway. He could see how Rural Route 4 cut through a corner of one lot, leaving a good-sized, flat field on the east side of the road. The small corner must be several acres in size, he figured.

Without getting off his bike, he scanned the field for signs of fresh-water springs. These were important, he knew, as they indicated a

14

good source of drinking water and irrigation water. He knew Mama had her heart set on planting a garden in the new place, wherever that turned out to be. A garden was most important.

He also figured that water running underground might connect to the nearby springs in Garden Springs, across Sunset Highway, where the truck farmers were known for their prolific gardens. He made a mental note to ask around about underground water in the area.

Looking closer, he saw that the larger part of the cut plat lay on the west side of the road — a rather steep hill covered with scrawny bushes and scrub pine, with traces of an overgrown road barely visible through the weeds. Unwilling to trespass on posted property, he decided against exploring it. Instead, he continued on his northward direction, pedaling past a deserted old stone house set back from the road, partially hidden in a tangle of weeds and overgrowth.

So far, the unpainted little house and the old stone house down the road were the only past or present signs of habitation along Route 4. If there were any people living on the side roads around here who worked in downtown Spokane, he thought to himself, they probably drove into town very early in the morning. No vehicles had passed him by, coming or going.

He pedaled along the dusty little road for a half-mile or so, paralleling the curve of the Rimrock. At the junction where a side road intersected Route 4 and branched off downhill through Indian Canyon, he got off his bike to have a rest. He wanted to view the landscape, smell the atmosphere, and listen to the sounds of the quiet countryside.

John found the air on the Rimrock so clean and pure he could recognize city sounds from five miles away: a piercing whistle from a train leaving the Spokane station, and the hourly chimes from the midtown clock tower.

In his immediate vicinity on the edge of the canyon, he could hear birdcalls drifting over the Rimrock. From a far-off farmyard, he could hear a rooster crowing and a dog barking. Now and then, he saw birds flying overhead to roost in the pine trees or nest in the meadow grass and bushes.

That evening, John's scouting report back to Papa was enthusiastically received, and immediately set wheels in motion.

Papa Announces Our Move
That night, Papa had a long talk with Mama, went to see the listed owner of the plats, gave notice to the landlord of the Third Avenue row-house, and made his announcement at the family supper table that night: "Kids, we've got two months to move into our new house!"

The timing was perfect: the June weather was fair and sunny, and the public schools had just let out for the summer. With the exception of nineteen-year-old brother David away at vocational school, we children would be free to help out with the move. Seventeen-year-old John, of course, would be helping with the house construction on the property he had discovered.

Mama discussed the responsibilities of us younger children. At fifteen, I would be expected to do my share, along with younger siblings Aaron *(13)* and Camilla *(11)*. Even little Pete *(7)* and Mike *(5)* would be expected to lend a hand. Furthermore, Mama emphasized, each of us would be responsible for looking after our own possessions, few as they were in those days.

Papa signed all the property papers, and speedily set about recruiting volunteers. He would need a lot of help to construct the new house.

Early the next morning, John set off once again on the long trip up the Sunset Grade to continue his plat assessment, now that it was legally permissible to explore all the selected property. Ignoring the flat meadow below where the house was to be built, he trekked up the hillside, curious to see where the old road led.

It was a stiff climb. At the crest of the hill, he found the ground gradually leveling off and the overgrown road coming to an end at the side of a large amphitheater-shaped pothole of solid basalt rock. From the number of stone slabs — some standing upright, a few with drilled holes, and some partially cut into the sides of the rock — the pothole obviously had once been a working stone quarry. Stands of scrub pine, clumps of grass, serviceberry bushes and weeds, all growing randomly among the rocks, were indications that the quarry had long ago fallen into disuse.

Retracing his steps to the rocky edge of the property that faced the road below, John climbed upon a flat chunk of basalt jutting out from the crest of the hill. From this vantage point, he could view the terrain for miles around; not far below him to the left he could see the old stone house down the road. Curiosity urged him on to see what kinds of stone the foundations were made of. A quick hike back down the hill and up the overgrown driveway of the stone house brought him close enough for a good look. He could see now that the foundations were, indeed, constructed from the local basalt rock.

Excited by this discovery, he wasted no time pedaling back to Papa's shop on Second Avenue with the good news: the foundations of the old house next door were basalt — of which there was an ample supply in the quarry on the hill.

Note 3. Basalt Rock: see Appendix.
Note 4. The Old Stone Quarry: see Appendix.

Digging the Foundations for the New House

Meanwhile, Papa was having good luck recruiting helpers to dig the foundations for our house. Although he himself had to keep on repairing leaky automobile radiators in his shop, every night after work he drove out to the construction site to bring building supplies and supervise the work. It was a race against time, with barely two months to the moving-out deadline.

Every night, Papa drove the Huppmobile out to the construction site with Mama and a picnic basket of supper for the hungry crew.

The hardiest volunteers now loaded chunks of basalt into a wooden cart and hooked it to Papa's old pick-up truck. They hauled the loads down from the quarry and positioned the rocks in the foundation area dug out for the basement of the house. Papa had learned how to mix the proper proportions of sand, water and lime into mortar, and this cemented the porous rock into a solid foundation.

As soon as the foundation was pronounced dry, Papa enlisted our Third Avenue neighbor, Mr. Dinwiddy, an experienced carpenter, to help with the next stages of construction: laying the flooring, nailing up the studs, erecting the joists, etc. With a basic flooring down, and a few walls up, there was something to walk on and some privacy for family members. It was now time, Papa declared, to move out from Third Avenue, "lock, stock and barrel!"

In the meantime, Mama had the foresight to talk with the foreman of the razing crew. She knew the minute we cleared out the old house that they would be tearing it down. "What are you going to do with the big picture window in the front room?" she asked the crew foreman. "And," she continued, "how about the leaded glass panes in the piano window?"

The foreman promised her that, rather than throwing the windows in the trash truck headed for the city dump, he would be happy to set them aside for her. So, after we had totally moved everything including ourselves out of the house, she and Papa made a special trip back to Third Avenue to pick up the antique windows and the picture window. "Much obliged!" she thanked the foreman.

Miraculously, the windows survived the rough truck ride up Sunset Highway and eventually — to Mama's great delight — were installed in our new house.

Papa also talked to the razing crew foreman about the cook-stove in the old house; if no one wanted it, he asked, would the crew please leave us the stove? It would be useful in the new house until we got an electric range. He knew that, otherwise, the old stove would have been left behind, being so heavy that the crew was unable to haul it, and no one else wanted it.

This frugal resourcefulness was typical of the swapping, bartering, and recycling of goods — as well as the countless acts of neighborly kindness engendered during the Depression Years. "In hard times, people have to learn to cope," was one of Mama's many mottos. "And everyone should lend a hand," she always added.

So Papa got a crew of volunteers together to haul Old Faithful, the cast-iron coal/wood-burning stove from our Third Avenue kitchen, out to the new building site. There, it was strategically positioned between two tall pines in a cleared area on the side of the construction. With its chimney attached to a wooden slat nailed securely to a tree, there was no danger of its collapsing in a high wind. When stoked with wood scraps, odd bits of lumber, kindling from the tree branches and twigs, Old Faithful heated up surprisingly well in the new location.

Later, as soon as the kitchen was plumbed and wired, Old Faithful was replaced by an electric range — a slightly chipped but otherwise brand-new floor model, sold cheaply at a discount store.

The REA *[Rural Electrification Administration]* had signed on Papa as a new subscriber some time before the actual moving day. They were already scheduled to put up electric light poles and run lines to the property, so that Papa and his volunteer work crew could then operate whatever equipment they needed at the building site. Also, we could have a few electric lights after sundown — until such time as the whole house was completely wired.

Water, of course, was an even more vital need. What good fortune for us that a well had been dug on the property long before we ever arrived on the scene in 1940!

Note 5. Who Else Had Lived Here Before Us? The Chinese Gardener, and the Japanese Gardeners: See Appendix.

Note 6. The Neighborhood "Little Red Schoolhouse" and the Japanese School Friends: see Appendix.

Building a House, Step by Step

Papa installed a small hand pump on the cased well under the tall pine trees, where we could pump up clear, cool water to serve everyone's needs during the construction. The separate processes of digging a septic tank far out in the field, and laying down connecting drain pipes and sewer pipes soon followed. Later, an electric pump was installed over the well casing, and eventually an electric water heater was wired in. We would have hot and cold running water! *Indoors!*

Each step in the construction of our house on Route 4 was greeted as a marvelous achievement: laying the foundation, laying down the first flooring, nailing up the wallboard, laying in the water pipes, electrical wiring, and plumbing in the washroom, bathroom and kitchen. Each step was a dramatic improvement in our standard of living.

The Free Basalt Rock Fireplace

No step, however, proved as traumatic as the installation of the fireplace. Papa had been especially keen on laying in a solid foundation for the fireplace. This was to be our only source of heat when the really cold weather set in, until such time as the house — and Papa's checkbook — would be ready for a furnace.

With John's discovery of the basalt quarry on the hill, Papa realized, happily, that he could utilize this free source of material for the fireplace. Unfortunately, no one on the crew of volunteer builders had any experience whatsoever with basalt, or had read anything about using basalt rock in fireplaces; so they simply proceeded to line the area at the base of the chimney with symmetrical pieces of basalt left over from the foundation rocks. When the final piece was fitted in place, everyone agreed that the rock slabs lining the fireplace "really looked very nice!" Papa was so pleased.

He himself laid the makings of the first fire, using crumpled newspaper, dry kindling wood, and a small pine log. With a ceremonial flourish, he struck a match, dropped it on the newspaper, and stood back to admire the bright flames igniting the paper, creeping up to the kindling wood, and thence to the pine log full of resinous pitch.

In no time at all, it seemed, the fireplace began emitting waves of delicious warmth. In fact, the fire heated up the basalt slabs so quickly, and to such a degree, that they started exploding and splintering into smithereens!

Hours later, after the basalt rock had cooled off, every bit of the handsome rock fireplace lining had to be removed. It was quickly replaced with a modern, "Superior Circulating Fireplace" guaranteed not to explode. This was the assurance of Charlie Siess, family friend and master house painter, who speedily installed it.

Moving Day
The days flew by in hurried preparation, and the two-month deadline was up. Ready or not, it was time to move into our new home.

According to schedule on Moving Day, Mama rode out in the first convoy with all the kitchen paraphernalia. First of all, she fired up Old Faithful, with its smoke stack securely wired to the pine trees next to the house, and prepared an enormous pot of chicken and dumplings. All morning long, it simmered there on the stovetop while, under Mama's direction, little helping hands brought a continual supply of fuel to feed it.

(Miraculously, on that stove that summer, Mama was to turn out enough beef stews, mashed potatoes, baked potatoes, baking powder biscuits, meatloaf, vegetable soup, fresh corn on the cob, cornbread, baked beans, gingerbread with whipped cream, rice pudding, and other hearty food for our hungry family and volunteer helpers until an electric range arrived early that fall.)

It took numerous trips on Moving Day to totally clear out of the old house. By Saturday night all our worldly possessions were in the new place: kitchenware, clothing, bedding, books, toys, pieces of furniture, boxes of keepsakes, battered suitcases, and *Grossvater*'s piano.

Just to make sure the piano was still in tune, and to see if music on the old piano would make me feel at home, I tried out a few beginners' songs that evening.

Anna Maria & Camilla with new neighbor
Yvonne Triplett, on the first night in the new house.

Everything still was topsy-turvy, of course, with all of our worldly possessions in a jumble around us that night, since there was nowhere to *put* anything. As Mama remarked, this was an unusual way of camping out, like nomads. True, we weren't actually living in a tent, but our house was still roofless. Papa said that as long as the weather held, we would be OK.

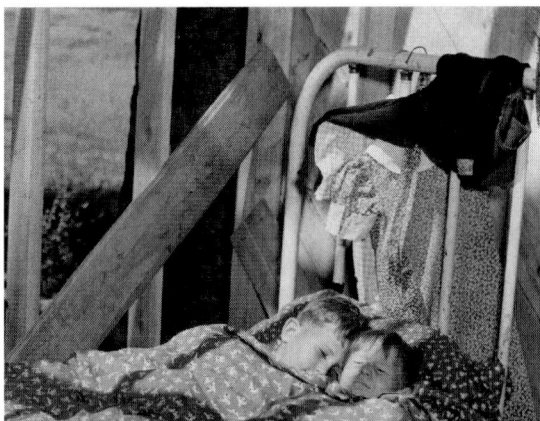

Pete and Mike pretend to sleep for the photographer.

Despite our makeshift sleeping spots, we all slept soundly until Pete and Mike's pet rooster Napoleon woke us all with his crowing.

We quickly learned basic rules for camping hygiene: how to pump water from the well into an enameled washbasin for washing hands and face, and brushing teeth with one cup of fresh water. We also learned how to dress behind a protective wall, out of sight of the road.

It was on this very first morning that two unexpected visitors arrived. The first was neighbor Yvonne, a young girl from the little house down in the hollow. Out of curiosity, she had walked over to silently watch all the activity in this previously uninhabited field.

The second visitor was a well-dressed young man who drove up in a roadster, parked in the field, and stepped out of his car holding a camera. He seemed not at all shy, but walked around the front, and instinctively found Mama at the other side of the house. Addressing her politely, "Good morning! Are you the lady of the house?" he introduced himself as a staff writer from *The Spokane Daily Chronicle* evening newspaper.

Mama, at the moment, was busily extracting a steaming pan of cornbread from the cast-iron cook stove situated between two tall pine trees by the side of the house. The visitor observed several young girls (my sister Camilla and myself) helping the cook, several older boys carrying wooden planks to the back of the house, and two younger boys peering out from behind a tree. It was a lively scene for such a pastoral Sunday morning.

"Yes. I'm Marie Jones," Mama responded. She looked around for Papa, who was discussing nails at the moment with Cousin Donald.

Cousin Donald oversees Aaron & Pete as they learn to nail the roof.
Young Pete was allowed to pound a few nails, just for the photo.
Note 7. Cousin Donald: see Appendix

Mama continued talking to the news reporter as she stoked the cook stove with lumber scraps. "My husband is Ethelbert Jones, proprietor of the Jones Radiator Shop on Second Avenue."

"Nice to meet you, Mrs. Jones," the young man said politely. "I can see you're busy, but would you mind a few questions?" he asked in his well-mannered voice.

"I guess not," Mama answered, in an equally gracious tone, giving directions to us girls to take plates and forks to the makeshift plank table at the back, while she cut the cornbread into large chunks. "We're just moving into our new house, you see."

"Yes, I see," the young man smiled. "I must say, I've seen a lot of people move into a new house, but never before it was finished. Without even a roof on!"

"Well, we wanted to move as soon as possible, while the weather was still clement. . . . Coffee?" She picked up a coffee mug from an open box, and filled it from the blue enamel coffee pot percolating on the back of the stove.

"Thank you, don't mind if I do," he smiled as she handed him the mugful of hot coffee, and a slab of buttered cornbread on a dessert plate.

Mama cooking breakfast the first morning

At her signal to the two boys, they brought out wooden chairs and placed them near the plank table. "So, how did you find us, if I may ask?" said Mama, fishing around in the open box for the condensed milk, sugar cubes, and spoons.

"I was taking my girlfriend for a Saturday night ride along Rimrock Drive over there." He waved in the direction of the canyon. "It's our favorite spot. Such a scenic view at night!"

"Yes, very scenic," murmured Mama.

"And then we heard *piano music!* I thought that strange, since I had never ever seen a single house along this road. I just *had* to come here in the daylight to see if I'd been hearing things!"

"Oh, your hearing is all right. My daughter Anna Maria was trying out the piano last night, and since there aren't any walls on that side yet, the sound just floats right out into the atmosphere!"

The reporter begged permission to take a few pictures, first posing my sister Camilla and me, along with neighbor Yvonne, in a trio at the piano.

By this time, Papa had finished discussing roofing nails with Cousin Donald, and came over to introduce himself. He explained that with the exception of the plumbing and bathroom utilities, he and members of the family along with a few friends were doing the building. And thanks to the REA, the refrigerator and washing machine were functioning perfectly. "We always wanted to build a home in the country, and still be close to the city," Papa told the reporter. "Here we have 20 acres that Mrs. Jones calls "Rocky Acres." He chuckled at the folksy name.

Note 8. Naming the Place "Rocky Acres." See Appendix.

Papa was enjoying his talk with the newspaper reporter. "Yes, there are deer just a stone's throw away, also quail, Chinese pheasants, and partridges in the field. And we hear coyotes at night.

We plan to develop the house a lot in the next year or two. Right now, we have a 74-foot cased well with good water. As soon as we get an electric pump, we will be able to irrigate a garden in this good soil."

The reporter carefully noted Papa's comments in his notebook, took more photos, thanked us all, and drove off in his little sports car.

Not long after this unexpected visit, an exciting, full-page spread appeared in *The Spokane Daily Chronicle Sunday edition*: **"Joneses Enjoy Open-Air Home."** The work on the house proceeded full speed ahead, before the cold blasts of winter arrived.

24

Master carpenter, Mr. Dinwiddie, has a motto: "Measure twice, cut once!"

Mama, Pete, Mickey & Aaron with Daniel Spaniel, by the wooden cart that gets hitched to a truck and hauls rock from the quarry on the hill.

Mama had rescued this antique leaded-pane piano window from the old house before the moving crew could trash it. Eventually it graced the family piano Grandfather Eggert Harms had bought from a traveling piano dealer in 1900.

EPILOGUE *Before the autumn rains set in, and the winter snows fell, the walls of the house had been plaster-boarded, the rafters were secured, temporary tar paper roofing was laid down, and the Superior Fireplace was functioning on a plentiful supply of broken tree limbs and chunks of pine logs.*

In time, further improvements were made and celebrated: a brand-new electric range replaced Old Faithful, which had served its final days under the pines and was eventually hauled off for scrap iron. Linoleum was laid down, and built-in cupboards were made for the kitchen. Papa himself tiled the sink board.

An electric pump was installed over the cased well, and the floor was laid in concrete. A bathroom with utilities in one corner was installed, and a drainage hole in another corner allowed wastewater to drain from the washing machine into the septic tank situated far out in the field. Then, after much study and consultation with various acquaintances, Papa devised an ingenious sawdust-burning furnace in the basement. This complicated project required a careful examination of the house layout before installing sheet-metal heating ducts upstairs and downstairs.

Note 9. Installing Heating Ducts for Papa's Sawdust Furnace. See Appendix.

Papa Passes Away

Sadly, Papa never got to see the completion of his house at Rocky Acres. Stricken with pneumonia, he passed away in Sacred Heart Hospital in Spokane, 1949, but his ingenious sawdust furnace heated the house for a number of years after his passing. By that time, my brother Aaron, now well trained in heating and cooling systems, installed a modern oil furnace for Mama.

When brother David returned home a trained electrician, he thoroughly checked all the house wiring to bring it up to code, and installed modern bathroom fixtures downstairs. He also made a plate railing around the ceiling near the picture window, for Mama's precious collection of antique glass bottles. She especially liked the effect of the fluorescent ceiling light that illuminated the bottles "with all the soft colors of a stained glass window," she once remarked.

When brother Michael came home on military leave a few years later, he installed an upstairs bathroom with a shower stall; built bookcases for Mama's detective stories; and designed decorative ceiling beams in the library corner.

As the years went by, Mama's picture window from Third Avenue gradually acquired an amazing collection of potted plants on the side shelves, its tendrils curling and interlacing around the window with a framework of greenery, greeting visitors as they entered the front door.

The Children Grow up and Leave Rocky Acres

Quite naturally, the children in the family eventually left Rocky Acres, affected in one way or another by World War II and its aftermath:

*   ***David** enlisted in the Army, and on his return married Rosemary Nason. In time, he owned a gardening store in northwest Spokane, but the couple built their home in the piney woods west of Spokane, where they lived for many years. They had a son, Evan, and a daughter, Janene.*

*   ***Anna Maria** worked her way through college to become a teacher, married Selahattin Malkoc, an engineering student from the Black Sea. They went to live in the oilfields in southeastern Turkey, and had five children: Hikmet, Cemile (died in infancy), Timur, Kâmuran, and Melike.*

    Sela died at age 43 in a traffic accident. Anna Maria and her children all live now in the Puget Sound area: in Edmonds, Mukilteo, Aberdeen, and Seattle.

Aaron Joseph enlisted in the Marines, later married Nona Paschek. Aaron trained and worked in air-conditioning/heating installation. Together, Aaron and Nona built a house on Grove Road (parallel to Basalt Drive). They had seven children: Theresa Maria, Christina Ann, Kathleen Elizabeth, Stephen Griffith, Stephanie Ursula, Megan Elin, and Michael Anton, who all live in Washington state.

Camilla worked her way through college, and married Wallace Phillipson when he returned from military tours. Wally became a steel construction foreman; Camilla returned to college to become a Washington State social worker. Together, they designed, built and lived in an A-frame house on Lake Coeur d'Alene in Idaho. They had four children: Andrew Paul, Matthew Dana, Marie Joy, and Sara Amy.

Now retired "Snowbirds," Camilla and Wally winter in Surprise AZ, and summer in Spokane WA.

Simeon Peter (Pete) enlisted in the Naval Air Corps, then operated his own radiator repair shop in California, later moved to Spokane. Now retired, he lives in Spokane Valley.

Michael Harris (Mike) enlisted in the Army, served in Korea and in the Peace Corps in Venezuela, went to Japan to teach English. There he met and married Miyako Tada, also an English teacher. They had a daughter Karen Tada, an artist, and a son, Ryuto Tada, now in university, and all living in Japan. Mike's hobby is building sail boats, one boat at a time.

John Harms was the exception to his brothers. As a result of gravely serious ear surgery in early childhood, he was ineligible to enlist during WW II. Instead, he worked with Papa in his radiator shop, repairing the enormous US Army trucks from Geiger Field. After Papa died in 1949, John took over the Jones Radiator Shop and operated it for many years.

John married Joyce McBride, and they built a home on the hill above the original Rocky Acres house. They had six children: John Curtis, Martha Ann, Jeffrey Burton, Thomas Reed, Wendy Ruth and Barry Russell.

Whatever Happened to the House?

Mama bequeathed the original Rocky Acres house to Simeon Peter and Michael, who had no homes of their own. Mike, in Japan, sold his share to Pete in California. He, in turn, sold both shares to Anna Maria, who also had no home of her own.

She retired in 1990, moved into the Rocky Acres house, had major repairs done, and a new well drilled. For nearly a decade, she taught English in a nearby women's college for Japanese students. Because her children preferred to live in the Seattle-Puget Sound area, she reluctantly sold the house and moved near them.

The original house has since passed into other hands, but John and Joyce still live in their cherished home by the rock quarry overlooking the older house below, on the road now officially listed as Basalt Drive.

4

PAPA *and the* PARKER HOUSE ROLLS
Rocky Acres, Spokane, Washington 1946

PROLOGUE   As a budding teenager with a critical eye, I considered our new neighbor, Mrs. Stolz, a really beautiful woman. Moreover, I admired her quiet sense of style. Whenever she came to answer the door in the old stone house down the road, she was never in hair curlers or an old bathrobe, but was always neatly dressed and groomed. Once, she remarked to me that though she had no children, she had an active social life, and always liked to be "prepared."

This was quite in contrast to Mama, who came from a large family, had seven lively children, and no social life. Mama usually did all her cleaning, cooking, laundry, and gardening while wearing old bib overalls. When finished with her daily chores, she would bathe and put on a clean, cotton-print housedress, and brush her long hair into a fresh coil atop her head, skewering it with tortoise-shell hairpins.

Yet, somehow, these two disparate types established warm, neighborly relations, and discovered a mutual appreciation of cooking and baking. Their interest evolved into a kind of swapping arrangement to test new recipes from the daily paper.

From time to time, Mama would ask one of us children to take a sample jar of delicate green mint jelly, golden quince jam, or crisp bread-and-butter pickles to Mrs. Stolz, with a note requesting her comments. With the exception of the sugar Mama used in the preparation, her ingredients almost always came from her own garden.

From time to time, Mrs. Stolz would bring over a different kind of bread or pie, to see what Mama thought of the latest recipes from the daily newspaper.

One day, our neighbor brought over a baking pan full of light and airy dinner rolls. They were made with yeast, she told Mama. After the dough had risen, she had kneaded and shaped it into small rolls, folded them over lightly, and browned them to perfection in the oven.

She explained that sometime in the 1870's, the baking chef in Boston's posh Parker House Hotel gave permission for their dinner rolls' recipe to be printed in a local newspaper. It was soon picked up and reprinted in newspapers throughout the U.S. During the 1930's Depression years and WWII, however, sugar was rationed and there were shortages of white flour, yeast, and butter. Patriotic housewives made no dinner rolls, pies, cakes, cookies, or donuts. People saved up their sugar rations to bake cakes only for very special occasions.

Now in post-war Spokane, Washington, Parker House rolls once again became popular, especially at dinner parties. No elegant dinner table was considered complete without them.

On the evening of this story, as I recall, my sister Camilla and I helped set the supper table, bringing in plates, cutlery, the butter dish, and a pot of apple butter. Mama came in to fill our plates with steaming vegetable-beef stew. It was nourishing, of course, but not exciting fare.

Then Mama came back to the table with a large plate of hot dinner rolls, announcing that they were Parker House rolls from Mrs. Stolz, our new neighbor in the stone house. From her tone of voice, I could tell Mama considered them something *special*. As usual, she had passed the plate to Papa first.

"Ah," he sighed after finishing off a roll with his stew. "The *best* Parker House roll I have *ever* eaten! In my whole *life!*" Reaching for another, he raved on. "They would win a blue ribbon prize *any*where, *any* day!"

Now, Mama, by nature, was a quiet, modest person. In her opinion, this kind of praise was fulsome and overdone. Though she held her tongue, as usual, Papa's extravagant compliments sparked a competitive spirit deep within her. Like the Biblical prophet who went unrecognized in his own land, Mama *knew* that despite the wartime shortages during the Depression, she had achieved some culinary successes herself, but she had never ever received any compliments at all. She decided it was time to teach Papa a lesson.

The next time Papa took Mama shopping at Weiners' Family grocery store on Third Avenue, he had to wait while she stocked up on baking ingredients, enough to last for quite a while.

"That took you longer than usual," remarked Papa.

"Well, yes. I decided I needed some kitchen supplies." And she let it go at that.

Her next step was to choose a weekday when the house would be empty and there would be no interruptions. It was important to concentrate on measuring and mixing the various ingredients, timing each step as directed in her neighbor's recipe notes. After a quick phone call next door to check on the pre-arranged time, Mama bundled up everything into a large basket, covered it carefully, and took the path across the field to the old stone house. At her brisk knock, the door was opened quickly with a short exchange of greetings. She put her basket on the kitchen table, together with the penciled notes and the oven timer. With a hurried nod and a smile, she was out of the door and back down the path through the field to her own kitchen in a matter of minutes. Mama's next task was to check on the roast beef in her oven, which needed to cook until it was "tender as a woman's heart." This would take a few more hours.

So, the afternoon wore on and the smaller children began drifting in from the neighborhood one-room schoolhouse, a mile or so down the road. We older children walked from our high school in town to Papa's shop, only a few blocks away. Papa usually had a chore for John to do, and I always had my school assignments to work on until five o'clock. Then Papa closed up shop and we all rode home with him in his truck. At home, everyone had odd chores, or homework, until it was time for supper.

On this particular evening, Mama put a fresh cloth on the round oak dinner table, and opened a jar of apricot jam she'd made from the apricots in her garden.

When it was time for us girls to set the table, and for the roast to come out of the oven, Mama sent Aaron out the back door to "pick up something from the neighbor." Camilla and I brought steaming bowls of garden-fresh vegetables to the table; Mama brought in the sizzling roast on its platter and placed it in front of Papa. As he began to slice the roast beef, I remember, he had a happy smile on his face. Mama called us all to the table.

"Where's Aaron?" Camilla asked.

"He'll be here," said Mama. "Please sit down." And sure enough, a minute later, Aaron was at the door, carrying a covered basket carefully with both hands.

"I brought these from Mrs. Stolz's house," he said proudly, placing a plate of dinner rolls in front of Papa.

"Ah," smiled Papa, "Mrs. Stolz's Parker House rolls! They win a blue ribbon in *my* book!" He helped himself to a slice of roast beef, and buttered a hot Parker House roll.

It was some time before Papa made any reference at all to Mrs. Stolz's special dinner rolls. At the supper table one evening, he mentioned rather wistfully how delicious the last Parker House rolls were — the ones Aaron had brought over that time. It was Papa's opinion that they were perhaps even flakier than the ones before.

"Is that *so*?" murmured Mama, reaching for the ladle of the soup tureen, while deftly changing the subject. "Care for another chicken leg? And another dumpling, perhaps?"

Marie Harms Jones & Ethelbert Jones c 1945

EPILOGUE *Although I was not around when the truth came out, if it ever really did, I know it was not in Mama's nature to crow over her victory. Just knowing that she had fooled Papa into thinking Mrs. Stolz had made the last batch of Parker House rolls was satisfaction enough for her. It was deliciously ironic.*

I imagine at some point her charming neighbor must have asked her privately for feedback: "Well, Mrs. Jones, what were the comments about your Parker House Rolls?"

And, I can just imagine Mama responding with a lift of her left eyebrow and that little smirky smile: "Well, Mrs. Stolz, I believe I won a blue ribbon!"

Camilla, Marie Harms Jones & Anna Maria c 1946

5

FLOATING TURKISH CARPETS
Ankara, Turkey 1964

PROLOGUE   One day, I came home from my English classes at the Gazi Teacher Training Institute in Ankara quite late in the afternoon.

I never worried about the children being left alone, because Münire, my favorite Gazi student, was staying with us and she always got home before the children. She helped with their homework and was a wonderful Big Sister to them, always resourceful and utterly dependable.

Rather than using my key to enter the apartment that day, I rang the bell and waited. I had decided to make it my habit to alert the household, because I never knew quite what to expect when I walked in.

When Münire opened the door, she was standing with my children, looking unusually serious, I thought at first glance. In fact, I slowly realized, they were *all* looking serious: my son Timur, nine; and my two younger girls: Kâmuran, eight; and Melike, still in the kindergarten for six-year-olds. (*My eldest daughter Hikmet, 13, was in Esenis Private Boarding School in Istanbul at the time.*)

This unusually formal welcome also struck me as especially *odd*; I had a fleeting impression of a drillmaster with his assembled troops, prepared for a review. Instinctively, I glanced about our spacious and sunny living room, and the hallway with doors leading to the bedrooms. Everything seemed in order. The polished parquet floors glistened in the afternoon sun, the ornate designs in the new Turkish rugs stood out in pristine patterns, as if just lifted from their looms. In fact, everything appeared to be neat as a pin, in spick-and-span order.

But no one spoke, not even to greet me. All four stood waiting, in silence. It was weird, and I looked around again in puzzlement: *What is wrong with this picture? Had I forgotten an important date? Was I late for something? Should I have brought a treat home with me today?*

Another minute or so passed. I couldn't stand the silence and I had to break it. "Münire, how *are* you? How are *all* of you*?*"

"Fine, thank you, Mrs. Malkoç," she replied in her polite and careful English. "Everyone is fine. Every*thing* is fine, now."

So, I was gathering from her hesitant tone of voice that something *had* happened. This was hard to imagine. Everything *looked* perfectly fine, nothing broken, that I could see, or burned. Then, *What is it?* I took a deep breath.

"Did something *happen*, Münire? Are you *all right?* Are the children *all right?"*

"We're *all* alright, Mrs. Malkoç. It's, well, you see, I'm sorry, something *did* happen, but it's all right now." She was stammering for words not in her usual English-lesson vocabulary.

It was at this point that Kâmuran silently sank to the floor and lay in a crumpled heap. So stunned that I couldn't take in the whole scene immediately, I felt as if I were moving in slow motion to pick her up, but Münire was already lifting her head, and Timur was already bringing her a cup of water. Melike was standing stock-still, apparently waiting for instruction.

"Let's all sit down, children," I said, as Münire and I walked Kâmuran to the sofa to lie down.

Once everyone was seated comfortably, I looked at Münire, who was usually calm in a crisis. "Münire? Can you tell me what is *wrong*?"

On the verge of tears, my favorite student burst out: "It was the *water* shortage this morning, Mrs. Malkoç! We were going to wash our hands and face and we tried *all* the faucets, but there was no *water*!"

"Yes, I know," I said. "There wasn't a drop of water at all when I left this morning. That's a problem here in Ankara. There's not enough water sometimes, so the City has to turn the water off now and then. You all know that."

Münire tried to offer her explanation. "Yes, Mrs. Malkoç. We all know that, so we all went off to school after you left this morning, and — "

She was still having great difficulty forming the unfamiliar words, and Timur stepped in. "I'm sorry, Mother, the problem was that, well, we *forgot* to turn off the faucets before we left — "

"So, when the water came on," Münire tried again, "all the faucets were already on, and — "

"A *lot* of water came out," piped up Timur. "A *lot*, Mother!"

I was slowly beginning to get the picture, but the thought of our brand-new apartment, with hardwood parquet floors in the spacious living room, the brand-new hand-made carpets, all deluged under gushing water was too horrible to contemplate.

Münire was still struggling to fight back tears and compose herself. Clearly, she felt responsible for reporting the afternoon's catastrophe: "When we opened the door, it looked like a *lake,* Mrs. Malkoç! I called the janitor and the neighbors. They all came to help sweep the water out of the apartment, and off the balcony."

Timur chimed in again. "Yes, the rugs were *swimming* in a *huge* lake, Mother! But the neighbors all came and hung the big rugs over the balcony railings. They dried in the sun. They're all dry now."

"The janitor says that the wood floors are all right." added Münire.

"Well, children," I said, with a philosophical sigh, "that's a lesson to all of us, isn't it?" They all solemnly nodded in agreement. "The last ones to leave in the morning should check to see that all the faucets are turned off. Let's make that a rule," I cautioned them, giving each one a hug and a kiss.

EPILOGUE Years later, in reminiscing about that apartment in Ankara — the one I'd bought with the insurance compensation after my husband's fatal road accident in 1963 — I had an epiphany.

Sela's heart's desire had been to buy a car in Holland on his return from a training trip to the U.S; his plan was to sell the new car and use the proceeds as a down payment on an apartment for us in Ankara. As it turned out, ironically, when I decided to buy an apartment where the children and I could live after he died, it was his life insurance that paid for it.

In further reminiscing, I recalled that catastrophic morning I left for classes early, and then my young children went off to school during a water shortage in Ankara. In hopes of getting water for washing, they had turned on every faucet in the new apartment: in the bathtub, the bidet, and the washbasin — all in the large bathroom; then in the separate Turkish toilet; and in the sink in the kitchen. That was a lot of open faucets.

Then the children left for school without remembering to turn off the faucets. Later in the day, of course, when the city water came back on, all the faucets gushed water until the children returned home and shut them off. . . .

For various reasons unconnected to the flood, I sold the apartment the following year, and my children and I left Turkey to live in the States. At dinner one quiet evening in Seattle, Washington, we were recalling the past year in Ankara.

"Mother," said Melike the youngest, who was remembering the afternoon of the calamity, "I was so sorry about flooding our apartment. We were responsible, but we didn't apologize, because we couldn't even talk about it!"

Then, using a new expression she'd just learned in English, she added, "We were <u>scared stiff</u>!"

6

RICH WHITMAN'S DAY SCHOOL
And What I Learned There
Edmonds, Washington c 1965

PROLOGUE   *Altogether, 1965 was a year of many decisions for me. It was three years after my husband Selahattin ("Sela") died, and when the Georgetown University English Program in Ankara ended its contract. That same year, my English-teaching job at Gazi Teacher Training Institute in Ankara phased out quite unexpectedly.*

Some of us teachers were offered positions in other places; I was visited and interviewed by a kindly professor from The American University in Beirut. He later wrote me saying, regretfully, that his university required a Master's degree. He would, however, be delighted to hire me as soon as I had earned the requisite degree.

After Sela's death, I knew it was important to recognize opportunities when they came along. I saw these separate events as "handwriting on the wall" signs telling me it was time to leave Turkey and return to the States. It seemed logical, even imperative, that I return to university to study linguistics, and get a teaching degree while I was still comparatively young and energetic. I had to make this effort now, in order to earn enough to sufficiently support my growing family. I knew I'd never be able to afford airfare so we could all visit my mother in Washington state; the thought of years of scraping by on a scant widow's pension and the children's insurance money was too bleak a picture to contemplate. For a number of reasons, then, I decided to move back to the States.

It was a most difficult decision to make. After living a hectic decade in the southeastern oilfields near the Tigris River, where Sela had been a government petroleum engineer, and then an active five years in the bustling capital of Ankara, Turkey had become my second home. Returning to the U.S. would mean leaving many dear friends; even more important to me was leaving Sela's family. Both his parents had passed away, but over the years, my three brothers-in-law and two sisters-in-law, with their spouses, children, and grandchildren, had endeared themselves to my heart.

I talked to teaching colleagues at the Georgetown English Language Program in Ankara about degree programs in the U.S. where I could study to qualify for teaching in a university. I wrote letters to various friends asking them for suggestions about courses, teaching jobs, and schools for my children. At night, in my half-dreams, I wrestled with different scenarios.

Finally, I hit on the idea of asking my Gazi student, Münire, if she would come along with us to the States, where I could help her enroll in a nearby women's college, and she could help me with the children. They all loved her dearly, she herself was overjoyed at the prospect, and her whole family was in happy agreement. According to my plan, we would all live with my mother in her house and garden out in the countryside on the outskirts of Spokane. My mother also was in happy agreement with the plan: my children would go to local schools, and help with the house chores; Münire would study for an English-teaching degree; I would look for a school offering linguistics and ESL (English as a Second Language) courses. We would all be taking classes, and doing our homework in the evenings. It would be a great learning environment. We were all planning happily for the future, in a new life together in my hometown.

By a cruelly bizarre twist of fate, that whole wonderful plan fell through. Strangely, Munire never received a response from the school in my hometown where I had hoped to enroll her. So, I had to rethink how to manage a day job somewhere else, oversee the children, and take university courses in the evenings. I was in a quandary again, but I couldn't give up at this point; I had to keep moving ahead. So I wrote letters to various stateside friends about my revised plans and asked them for more advice.

In the meantime, with the help of my old friend and neighbor Perihan Turgay, an experienced attorney, I sold my new apartment in Ankara for cash, and invested half the amount in shares of the government's new iron-and-steel mill. The remainder was enough to pay for our travel from Turkey to Spokane, and cover our schooling for the coming transition year. The following few months passed like a dream; we were all busy making lists, packing up, saying goodbye to relatives, friends, and neighbors in Ankara.

On departure day, the children and I boarded a train to Istanbul for more farewells. From there we took an international bus to Munich; laid over two days waiting for a train connection to Icelandic Air in Luxembourg; were met by friend Barbara Chidsey from Ankara College, who now lived in New York. We spent the night at her house, and she took us out to La Guardia airport for the last leg of our trip: by plane via Los Angeles to Spokane. All on cut-rate tickets, arranged by travel-agency friends.

That first summer in Spokane was an exciting time for us. We visited my mother and siblings; my children met their aunts, uncles, and cousins. Together, we visited dear neighbors and family friends.

To especially honor their grandmother, my little "Folk-Dancing Four" put on their Turkish costumes with floating scarves, colorful baggy pants, bright cummerbunds and fez-like toques, and performed their regional dances outdoors in my brother Aaron's garden. As Mama sat in her comfortable garden chair, the children sang and skipped across the green lawn in front of her, like creatures from a Far-Eastern fairy tale. Mama was in a state of blissful elation.

Thirteen-year-old Hikmet, who had visited Spokane only two years before, was the self-appointed bilingual representative for the group. She translated effortlessly, and cleared up many mysteries for her younger siblings: 9-year-old brother Timur, 8-year-old sister Kâmuran, and 5-year-old sister Melike. For them, everything seemed marvelously "modern" at Grandmother's. They would quietly discuss details amongst themselves, and ask Hikmet questions about things not immediately comprehensible — all in Turkish, of course.

I was concerned about how the three would adjust to school in the fall, only a few months away. While shopping one day at the supermarket, I found a rack of "Fun Activities for Young Children" books, graded by age and containing matching-picture puzzles, easy-to-fill-in-the-blank stories with clues, and illustrated riddles. I selected three books, and bought three pencils with erasers.

"Try these for fun," I said as I distributed them. "When you finish your book, you'll win a dollar!" Then I sat down with Melike to explain how to solve an easy matching-puzzle, but soon realized that Melike hadn't yet reached "reading readiness" stage. Timur, on the other hand, for whom one whole American dollar was an enormous incentive, won his dollar in less than a week. Kâmuran, a deliberate and careful reader, took somewhat longer to start reading in English.

As it turned out, I needn't have despaired at their progress in learning to speak English. I should have known that given time, Nature would take its course. Small children strive to resemble their peers or playmates; it's a natural instinct. By September, when it was time to leave the comfort and security of Grandmother's house to look for schools and a job for me in Seattle, the three younger children were no longer speaking Turkish with each other, but English.

My old high school friend, Liz Hadley, who, like myself, was also recently widowed, now lived in Seattle. When we arrived at the SEATAC (Seattle/Tacoma) airport, Liz was there to meet us.

She'd already found us a rental house, she told me, right across the street from her house! Also, she had information about a private elementary school I might consider for my children. "You could call it a day school for children of working mothers," she said. "I send my daughter Susan there because the school bus picks her up at the door here before I go off to work in the morning, and drops her off here after I get home in the afternoon."

Liz was teaching Latin in a Seattle high school, so the day-school hours were perfectly compatible for her. They would be compatible for me, too, as I was enrolling in day courses at the U. of Washington. I'd decided to study advanced Turkish grammar to eventually qualify as a translator/interpreter.

My next move, then, was to enroll the children in the same day school as little Susan. Naturally, I was extremely happy to learn about the convenient bus service. I was also relieved to learn that that the minimum age for baby sitters in the state of Washington was 12 years. This meant that Hikmet, already over 13, was legally old enough to serve as baby sitter for her younger brother and sisters until I returned home from the University by bus each day. I considered her a responsible young teen-ager, capable of looking after her siblings when necessary. Additionally, I was especially keen to put the children in the private school for the first year, because they urgently needed to learn to read and write English. (English spelling is such a bugaboo for new readers!)

For all these reasons, the day school seemed like a good choice. I don't know how I could have managed that first year, otherwise.

Rich Whitman, owner of the day school, had been an ambulance driver in France during World War I. In all his contacts with wounded soldiers on both sides of the fence, he had learned enough rudimentary German to be convinced that every American schoolchild should learn a foreign language. In his school, he himself taught the beginning German classes. "It's a valuable asset, and opens windows on your horizon."

He told me all this during an interview in his Director's Office. Who was I, of all people, to disagree with him? I'd had first-hand experiences with foreign-language learning and culture shock for the past 15 years!

"I agree with you two hundred percent," I smiled, and briefly explained that I'd just arrived from Turkey with my four children, and hoped to enroll them in his school for a year. My children *understand* English, I told him, because I've always spoken to them in English, but they always respond in Turkish. People seemed surprised to hear this, but it seems natural to me because children always understand their mother — as long as she always speaks the same language to them from birth, which I always do.

They're now in a transition phase, I further explained. In Turkey, they've always spoken to each other in Turkish, and now they're changing to speaking in English. But they aren't *fluent* in English yet. In addition, they can't *read* or *write* English at all. Except my oldest daughter, who is bilingual, I added.

From time to time, Mr. Whitman nodded and looked thoughtful, trying to picture this unusual, linguistic to-and-fro. "I see," he would mutter. I'm not sure that he did, really; he just changed the subject. "Another thing I'm convinced of is the value of giving each child opportunities for speaking in public. I try to promote this in my school."

Again, I couldn't agree with him more. I asked, "How do you go about giving the children opportunities?"

"I write a Pageant or Show twice a year, and every child takes part in two little groups on their class level. They learn to memorize their lines and songs, and practice their parts in public. Some of my friends in the U. of Washington music department help out by singing some of the adult parts. Then, at the end of each semester, we have a Show Night and all the parents come to see the children perform. We usually have several hundred people show up, and they're an enthusiastic audience!"

How all this could actually work out was a mystery to me, but it sounded exciting. I had always loved performing in school performances myself. In fact, being on stage has held a life-long allure for me. So, I was sold on the idea, and sold on the school, because I knew the children would not only be forced into *speaking* English, but also guided into *reading* and *writing* English.

Mr. Whitman went on to tell me about his school-busing system. "It goes like clockwork," he stated proudly. "We try to accommodate the children's bus times with their parents' work schedules, so no one is left out in the cold!"

He gave a chuckle at his little witticism. "Our office accountant," he continued, "will give you a list of tuition fees, rules and regulations, school terms, daily schedules, and telephone numbers. She's just around the corner there; her sign's on the door." He waved vaguely in a southerly direction, past the bookcases crammed with dictionaries and textbooks, some new and some dog-eared.

He gave another chuckle. "By the way, we offer discounts for additional children. And it's been a pleasure to meet you!"

We shook hands and I followed his vague wave out of the room into the office around the corner, where the accountant was sitting, waiting to enroll new pupils.

The days following enrollment in the Rich Whitman Elementary School classes have passed into a misty haze in my memory. My children were assigned to different rooms: one to a large room accommodating several grades at once, the others to small barrack-like Quonset huts (purchased from post-war surplus supply stores) that sat on the school grounds in Edmonds, about an hour's drive north of Seattle. *(Coincidentally, not far from where I am presently writing these memoirs, nearly a half century later.)*

The total enrollment at the Rich Whitman School may have been around 100 children at the time. This is a haphazard guess; it may have been more or less. I was never around to see children moving *en masse* from classroom to classroom, being intent on my own classroom attendance at the university, and doing my homework each evening.

What does remain vivid in my memory is the sight of ten bright yellow school buses all lined up in a precise row in the parking lot early one morning. The school's maintenance man stood at the front of the line with a stopwatch, holding a red starting flag. As he swooped his flag down, all ten drivers revved up their motors with military precision.

At his second signal, all ten drivers shifted gears, and one after the other, rolled out of the driveway and on toward their appointed destinations. They were off to pick up the individual pupils according to their scheduled timetables, from locations all over the greater Seattle area. Never having seen the buses bringing the pupils to the school in the morning, I couldn't begin to guess the number of passengers, or calculate the total school enrollment, but I was fascinated just watching the disciplined bus departure. It was an impressive sight.

Several months of busy days and weeks passed, including Columbus Day, Halloween, and Thanksgiving. On the night of the Christmas Pageant, I was nearly as excited as the twittering, giggling little children congregated offstage in the halls. Their piping voices could be heard laughing and shouting to each other as they waited for the beginning signal from Mr. Whitman.

In the meantime, parents and family members began filing into the auditorium, now full of several hundred folding chairs. Friends greeted friends and acquaintances and sat down to chat amiably until curtain call. Promptly at eight o'clock, a teacher rolled out an upright piano to stage left, positioned a music book on the piano rack, and sat down.

Without fanfare, Mr. Rich Whitman himself stepped out on center stage: tall and portly in a dark suit, wearing a green vinyl eyeshade in protection against the bright footlights, and carrying a thick script book in one hand and a folding chair in the other.

He first splayed the chair open so it read **DIRECTOR** in large letters on the back, bowed formally to the audience, and then sat down facing the stage, with his back to the spectators.

The weak scattering of applause indicated that the audience was well acquainted with the pageant protocol. They were holding their applause for the dramatic looking Master of Ceremonies, who appeared shortly amidst enthusiastic whistles and handclapping. His sweeping bow and smile, signals that the show was about to begin, stilled the applause. In a rich, melodious voice, he introduced himself and announced: "The Rich Whitman Annual Christmas Pageant!"

From his director's chair center stage, Director Whitman gave a quick wave of his hand, and announced in a low voice: "Group One!" The piano player struck up a rollicking tune, and the show began.

The little first-graders, all togged out in holiday finery, bravely marched out onto the stage. Each child sported some kind of antlers, wings, tails, or bunny ears to represent reindeer, chicks, puppies, ducklings, kittens, rabbits, and/or other adorable animal offspring. Despite their bobbling attachments, and precariously attached appendages, they managed to sing their happy little group song and bravely march off stage.

More piano segues signaled the next groups: little elves helping out in Santa's workshop, and awkward reindeer balancing their antlers and bearing big knobby bags of presents for good little children. Each group sang jolly, non-religious songs about the happy holiday season, and danced through a few simply choreographed steps.

Just as many of the other memories have dimmed, so have details of the program's scripted and choreographed segments. That there must have been a gentle storyline woven into the pageant was evident from the row of Mr. Whitman's friends from the UW music department; these talented back-up singers included a soprano, contralto, tenor, baritone, and a marvelously deep *basso*.

While I didn't quite catch the storyline, I did enjoy the singing, and I loved watching the children going through their paces. It was a special thrill to be able to see my own children participating in such a well-coordinated, delightful performance.

EPILOGUE *By 1985, "much water had flowed under many bridges," to re-coin an old expression. We had managed to get through the transition year moving from Turkey to the U.S. On reliable counsel, I was advised that a translating job would not pay enough to support my little family, so I decided against taking Turkish translation courses. Through the kindness of Dorothy Pedtke, an old friend from Ankara, I landed a job as abstractor-indexer and cataloger at the Center for Applied Linguistics in Washington DC, where Dorothy was working. (These were the years shortly before the advent of computers.)*

My CAL job lasted five years. During this time, my younger children completed elementary and middle schools, and I completed evening courses for a Master's degree in Applied Linguistics. When I was offered a Fulbright grant to teach English conversation classes in a Polish university, I found a co-ed boarding school in England for my son Timur and daughters Kâmuran and Melike. The school assured me my children could travel either by train or bus to Poland to spend the "long" holidays (summer and Christmas/New Year's) with me in Poland, or they could make arrangements to fly to visit our relatives in Turkey.

Hikmet, my bilingual eldest, had already finished high school, was living with relatives in Ankara, and had an office job at her father's old company. . . .

Several years later, with all of my children studying/working more or less on their own, I applied and was accepted into the Foreign Service as an English Teaching Officer in Washington DC. Eventually, I was sent by the U.S. Information Agency (now part of the U.S. State Department) on a four-year teaching assignment to Ankara. This was followed by a similar assignment to Warsaw.

It was there in Warsaw that I received an unusual call for assistance from my English-teaching friend, Ursula Peters at the American School.

She explained: "The Easter holiday is coming up, and I need a little play or story about the Easter Bunny, or something traditional like that — but not religious — for my pupils. It will help their English, and their parents can come and see how much English they are learning here." She added, "These children at the American School in Warsaw are from diplomats' families, mostly from non-English speaking countries. Do you know of any appropriate material I could use?"

At her question, I had an immediate flashback to the exciting success of Rich Whitman's Christmas Pageant two decades earlier. I was instantly inspired.

"Oh, Ursula," I responded without a moment's hesitation, "I'll write you a little play!" It just happened that in my free time that year, I was writing "Easy Plays in English," designed to involve all the students in conversational language practice, so I was in a play-writing mood. Ursula agreed to send me a list of the names and ages of the children in her English class.

In the meantime, I would think up a storyline and simple songs for the actors. The result was a scenario entitled, "Mr. Easter Bunny and His Helpers." The story dealt with the problems of finding and organizing volunteer helpers to gather eggs, then color and deliver them in time for the holiday. In the story, it was the little helpers who managed to save the day.

Remembering Rich Whitman's groups of "adorable animals," I came up with two groups, with enough parts for the dozen or so children in each:

Group 1 were spring flowers who helped the Easter Bunny color the eggs. In their song, the children described the flowers or animals they represented.

Group 2 were forest and field creatures who filled the baskets and carried them to every house. In their song, they described the tasks they were carrying out.

I wrote the words to suit the grammar according to the pupils' levels of English, and set the easy words to music — public-domain melodies already familiar to the children.

Ursula approved the script pages, made copies and assigned parts to each child. I had added a page of notes for entrances, exits, and photo opportunities between scenes ("photo-ops" being important to the parents and grandparents).

Ursula kept me informed of her pupils' progress, and showed me the role assignments. I asked why Mr. Bunny's part was assigned to a girl.

"She's the oldest and tallest in the group, and the most advanced in English. I think she can manage the role best."

"Then, change the role to Mrs. Bunny," I suggested. "Hmm. She has a Muslim name. Is she Turkish?"

"They speak Turkish. They're from Azerbaijan."

"I'd love to meet them! Can you please assure them the play is not at all religious?

50

Ursula promised to clarify this with the parents, in case they were concerned on this point. . . . Apparently, they were not concerned, it turned out, but were immensely proud that their daughter had the leading part, in English!

The evening of the Children's Program arrived, and once again, I was as excited as the little performers themselves. Ursula had reserved a front-row seat for me, so I was able to see every detail of the children's costumes stitched by their nervous mothers.

I thought the outfits were most cleverly designed and ornamented to represent the children's roles. Two flower costumes still stand out in my memory after all these years: the little Japanese girl's pansy costume in rich royal purple and gold, and the little Turkish girl's tulip costume in brilliant crimson, framed by emerald green leaves. The two looked like exquisitely delicate flowers in their hand-made outfits, and both performed beautifully, to the immense pleasure of their proud families.

"Rest in peace, Mr. Whitman," I breathed silently. "Thank you for your inspiration, and greetings from the American School in Warsaw!"

7

YOUNG TURKISH FOLK DANCERS
Washington, DC   c 1966-70

PROLOGUE *My husband Selahattin, a petroleum engineer in the Turkish Petroleum Company (TPAO), and I had lived for ten years in the oilfields in the southeastern region of Turkey before he was transferred to headquarters in Ankara. With our four children, we settled happily into a pleasant apartment in a residential neighborhood in the city.*

Tragically, he died the next year (1963) in a traffic accident while returning from a training trip abroad. My children and I remained in Ankara for several more years; they went to public schools there while I taught English at the Gazi Teacher Training Institute.

I then decided to return with my children to the U.S., where they could attend neighborhood schools, and I could work full time during the day, then take evening classes to earn a higher university degree.

There were countless tasks to attend to before packing up, saying goodbye to our many relatives and friends, and bidding farewell to Turkey. Not all the tasks were sad, however.

I remembered how delighted my mother had been to watch ten-year-old Hikmet folk dance when she and I had visited her several years earlier, so on several weekends, I asked my Gazi students if they would teach my children different dances from their own regions of Turkey. They turned out to be wonderful instructors, and were happy to instruct the children in a variety of interesting dances.

At the same time, I was inspired to ask my sisters-in-law, Nezihe and Güher, to help me assemble folk-dance costumes for my daughters and my son.

To make the girls' shalvars (baggy pants), their Aunt Nezihe chose beautiful satin brocades in varying stripes of brilliant crimson, emerald green, gold, and blue. Their Aunt Güher made each girl a full-sleeved white cotton blouse, hand-embroidered with dainty pink tulips and coral carnations.

At the Old Market in downtown Ankara, I bought large scarves, to be folded tightly as cummerbunds around their waists, and embroidered vests of varying colors. In addition, I found flowing silk scarves of scarlet, gold, and emerald green stripes, to be anchored down under their small pillbox-type hats. Sometimes, the girls liked to wear the softer, white muslin headscarves, so I found some squares edged with shiny sequins, and some with tiny dangling daisies. Finally, to complete their outfits, their Uncle Muammer picked out four pairs of hand-tooled slippers made of heavy red leather with turned-up toes, all in the right sizes.

Admittedly, the girls' outfits were a real mix of ethnic garments from different regions of Turkey, yet somehow they created a lovely impression of "Turkishness" when they were dressed and whirling around in singing circles.

On the other hand, Timur's special dance, the Zeybek, was typical of southwestern Anatolian villages. One Gazi student from this region volunteered to teach Timur this complicated, vigorous dance; the two practiced diligently for a number of weekends until Timur was finally pronounced "ready to perform." His swashbuckling costume consisted of a pair of short black velvet pants; a multicolored silk sash as a cummerbund, and a black velvet vest embroidered in gold thread. His very first men's style shirt was made of shiny white satin, with real cufflinks.

Each year, one of the loving aunts would send Timur a package with a larger-sized shalvar and a larger vest, to accommodate his growth spurts. For the girls, I would arrange for someone to send lengths of material for new shalvars as they outgrew their old ones, and Hikmet would find someone in the Turkish community in Washington DC to help cut out and sew up the simple garments.

For his Zeybek dance, Timur's headgear was a dark red felt fez, with a rolled-up striped scarf tied around the brim, and its fringed ends hanging down at a rakish angle. His fez was reminiscent of the hat his father Selahattin Malkoç had worn to primary school on the Black Sea (until President Atatürk established the Hat Law in the late 1920s, and the fez was abolished as everyday headgear in Turkey).

Timur was also given four hand-painted wooden spoons — a pair for each hand — that he learned to click sharply like castanets as he danced. His specialty move was to swoop down and curve one arm as he touched the ground on one knee, arching the other arm "high as an eagle," all the while clicking the spoons in rhythm with the drum beat.

Unlike his sisters, who sang accompanying songs as they danced, Timur's dance required regional music from a record player. It also required balance and coordination, dancing skill, and real finesse with the wooden spoons.

The only girls' dance that required anywhere near such expertise, in my opinion, was what they called the "Wedding Candles Dance" ("Çayda Çirag") from the eastern Elazig region. Most effectively viewed outside at nightfall, or in a darkened room, this dance required great care in managing the candles that the dancers were given to cup in their hands as they entered the dancing area. Slowly, singing the lovely melody in their high, sweet voices, they *rhythmically swooped the candles in their outstretched hands, moving them in gentle arcs as they advanced gracefully through the meadow or brook side — or wherever the wedding celebration was taking place.*

Maintaining an even tempo as they moved into a circle was the least of the dancers' worries: the fragile candle flames threatened to go out with any too-sudden movement, and an extinguished flame would create an immediately visible gap in the dancers' circle of candles. A worse threat, of course, was that any slight breeze might blow a tiny flame into contact with the gauzy fabric of the dancers' floating veils.

All threatened risks aside, this stately dance — when executed in slow and graceful movements, accompanied by their sweet soprano voices, and illuminated by the flickering candles — created an ethereally lovely scene. The young girls performed this dance rarely, and only under careful supervision.

Whenever the children were asked to dance, Hikmet would choreograph their program, usually opening with a group dance and first announcing the name and giving a few words of explanation: "This is the Harvest Dance. The dancers move in a circle. Their arm movements imitate the motions of cutting grain with long scythes, or grasping handfuls of grain with one hand, and cutting the sheaves with a short sickle."

The three girls together usually did the next number: "Çifteteli is a traditional wedding dance with a rather complicated rhythm. Turkish children learn this favorite dance at school."

Hikmet usually programmed her brother to follow with his specialty: "Timur will now perform the Zeybek, a village hero's energetic dance from the southwestern villages of Anatolia." Finally, an all-group dance would end the program.

On several occasions, Kâmuran added her own original and dramatic surprise. As the dancers completed the final circle and were taking a long, slow bow, she gently reached into her cummerbund and extracted a rolled-up, fine-spun Turkish flag by its corners (12 inches x 18 inches in size).

At the exact moment that the other dancers finished their bow, Kâmuran straightened up, simultaneously lifting her head and holding up the small flag. She stood there for a long, silent moment, holding aloft the brilliant red flag with its white crescent moon. Then she bowed to the audience again, and slowly exited with flag held high, the other dancers following in her wake.

*Kâmuran tries out a dramatic finale
with her Turkish flag.*

The applause was fervent, with a few older men wiping away a silent tear, remembering Selahattin, the children's father. Some had been Turkish Government scholarship students studying together with him in Germany in the 1940s. In 1945, when WWII ended, they were sent in a group to universities in the U.S. and then on to the newly established petroleum refining industry sites in southeastern Turkey. They were once referred to as part of the "new generation of Atatürk's children."

I thought Kâmuran's sense of timing and her sense of the dramatic quite surprising for a nine-year-old with no theatrical training. My one regret was that Mrs. Esenbel, the Ambassador's wife who had given the flag to the children after their first performance at the Turkish Embassy, never got to see one of Kâmuran's special exits. I believe she'd have been proud to see how dramatically the flag was displayed.

My children had a number of opportunities to folk dance during the five years we lived in Washington DC: not only at the Turkish Embassy, but at the American-Turkish Association functions, and at international programs in the children's schools.

I welcomed each invitation the children received, hoping that the folk dancing would help them develop self-confidence and poise, and give them a special sense of pride in their Turkish heritage and the legacy of their remarkable father who had died when they were still quite small. I also hoped their folk dancing would ease the transition to their new life in DC.

Happily, the schools they attended in the northwest corner of Washington, DC (Janney Elementary, Alice Deal Junior High, and Woodrow Wilson High) included children from around the world in their classes.

As a family, we soon made friends with members of ATA (the American-Turkish Association) and with my colleagues at CAL (the Center for Applied Linguistics), where I wrote abstracts and annotations for publications in linguistics and English as a foreign language.

Melike and Timur Malkoç demonstrate their wooden spoon "castanets" to Dr. Zeki Erim, president of the American-Turkish Association, in a celebration at the Washington Hilton Hotel in honor of the new Turkish Ambassador.

Appreciation Dinners with Turkish Entertainment   Once a year, the children and I would organize a special thank-you party for our kind and helpful friends at ATA, and then another party for my colleagues at CAL, to show appreciation for their many acts of kindness throughout the year. I mailed out a simple invitation: *"The children and I would like to invite you to a shish kebab dinner with baklava, Turkish coffee, and a dancing troop."*

Preparations for the dinner had to begin several days in advance:
First, I phoned in an order for a leg of lamb already cubed for shish kebab at the special grocery store that advertised "Deliveries to Your Door." It was scheduled to arrive after Hikmet was home from school, so she could marinate the meat and put it in the fridge. Two evenings before the dinner, on my way home from work, I'd get off the bus at the neighborhood Safeway supermarket on Wisconsin Avenue, and as prearranged, I'd meet the four children waiting with our two family shopping carts. We divvied up the shopping, with Hikmet and Melike taking one cart for the fresh vegetables and canned foods:
- Red and green onions, parsley, tomatoes, cucumbers, black olives, and fresh lemons *(for shepherds' salad);*
- Fine white rice, pine nuts, butter; and dried currants *(for pilav);*
- Prime olive oil, garlic *(for the salads);*
- Canned garbanzo beans, sesame oil *(for hummus);*
- Thin baguettes, or French bread *(for hummus dip).*

Timur and Kâmuran took one cart for special items:
- One can of finely ground Turkish coffee (*Melitta* brand);
- One box of *baklava* from a bakery on Wisconsin Avenue;
- 6 tall gold candles from a shop on Wisconsin Avenue;
- One gallon of Gallo Bros. red *Zinfandel*. (I had to buy this popular wine at a wine shop.)

Instead of always making shepherds' salad, I learned to make *tabuli*, a cracked wheat *bulgur* salad with lots of diced sweet onions, tomatoes, chopped parsley and other spring vegetables, olive oil and fresh lemon juice. It was always popular. When leg of lamb was out-of-season, I made Turkish meatballs, or cold sliced Circassian chicken with walnut sauce, another popular dish.

Preparation for these parties also meant a thorough Saturday-morning cleaning, dusting, and polishing all the copper, brass, and silver utensils. While the children were polishing, I prepared the food in the kitchen. After the four young polishers finished, the large copper tray had a warm rosy glow, the silver candlesticks gleamed, and the big brass brazier shone like pure gold. I set out the buffet table while the children were washing up and putting on their costumes. Then I dressed for the evening, and they rested upstairs until our guests arrived.

Depending on the size of the crowd, the children sometimes came down to greet guests and serve appetizers. Other times, they simply waited until everyone was seated with plates of food and I gave them a secret signal. Promptly, the quartet would begin singing in unison as they made a dramatic entrance at the top of the stairs. In their colorful regalia, they would slowly descend the narrow staircase and pause at the bottom for full impact on the audience, and for Hikmet to announce the name and origin of their opening dance.

The guests were happy to sit with buffet plates on their laps and leisurely sample the exotic dishes as they watched the twirling young singers. Sometimes after a dance, the children would politely take a food break themselves and mingle with the guests, regrouping for another dance or two, then making a final exit bow and departing the scene — amidst applause and cheers.

Although dancing in the home atmosphere was so comfortable for the children that they never experienced stage fright, neither did they feel so complacent and overconfident that their performances suffered from it. With Hikmet leading them, they always gave each performance their very best, no matter whether they were dancing for their Grandmother Jones in the garden in Spokane, Washington, or for the new Turkish Ambassador in the Hilton Hotel in Washington, DC.

Appearing on the "Claire and Coco Show" One of the highlights of my children's folk-dancing career was their appearance on the "Claire and Coco Show" children's program in Washington, DC in the 1960s.

Claire and her white poodle Coco

In the days before the advent of *Sesame Street, Mr. Rogers' Neighborhood,* and *Teletubbies,* Claire's daytime show was immensely popular with small children. This was due partly because she was such a beautiful and versatile talk-show hostess with a knack for hitting it off with children, but also because her standard-size white poodle, Coco, was an instant hit whenever or wherever they appeared together.

Popular Claire had a showman's gift for finding unusual and educationally interesting guests to interview, including children from the various embassies in DC. Although my children and I were not an "Embassy" family, Turkish Ambassador Esenbel's wife had suggested to Claire that my children might be appropriate visitors on her show. They had dual citizenship (two were born in Turkey), were bilingual, sang songs in Turkish as they danced, and wore beautiful costumes made by their aunts in Turkey.

So, at Mrs. Esenbel's behest, Claire called me one day to talk to me about the children. I told her I had three daughters and one son:

ages 14 to 7. They had learned many folk dances at school in Turkey, and had danced for their relatives, at their cousins' schools, and on *Captain Kangaroo's Program* in Spokane. Also at the Turkish Embassy and at the new Islamic Mosque in Washington DC on Children's Day.

She quickly penciled in an appointment on her calendar. I sensed, however, her reluctance at dealing with four children at once — unknown entities, as it were. Who knows when children will clam up, or refuse to take direction? So, trying not to sound like a doting mother, but more to reassure Claire, I said they all *enjoyed* dancing. Unfortunately, my eldest daughter, who did all the announcing, had special classes on the appointment day, but I reassured her my middle daughter would fill in as the announcer.

We arrived on time in Claire's small studio, where chairs were lined up in anticipation. She greeted us and smiled as she shook hands all around. "Have your children had any professional training for TV performances?" she asked during this preliminary interview.

I shook my head. "They learned their dances at regular school in Turkey, with all the other schoolchildren. Also from some of my students in the Teacher Training Institute there," I replied.

"Well," she smiled, "let's see what they can do. What is their first dance?"

I nodded at Kâmuran to make the introduction in English. "This dance is called '*Harman Dali.*' It's a harvest dance," she announced. "The villagers are cutting the ripe wheat and making bundles." She joined hands in a small circle with Timur and Melike, they sang/danced a short version of the dance and took a little bow. I gave Timur a slight signal as I handed Claire the record for her record player.

"My dance is called the *Zebek.*" Timur announced. "It's from southwestern Anatolia." He pulled his wooden spoons from his pocket, and as strains of the melancholy oboe merged with the rhythmic beat of the big drum, he clacked the spoons in tempo, beginning his heroic striding and swooping, down on one knee, up with one arm arched like an eagle.

Claire watched him intently for some minutes, and then cut the music off. She first congratulated the three on their performances before turning to me. "And you say they haven't had professional training?" She shook her head in disbelief. "They're *so* professional!"

She called several days later, with a set date for their appearance on her afternoon show. I couldn't leave work, but a kind friend arranged to pick the children up and bring them home. Another friend taped the program for us, so we could watch it at home the next evening. What a thrill it was to see my children on TV!

At the Walter Reed Army Hospital in Washington, DC. Sometime after their "Claire and Coco Show" performance, Timur made a serious announcement: "Mother, I'm not going to wear those short velvet pants any more! If my friends saw me, they would make fun of me!" I managed to persuade him to go along with Kâmuran and Melike to Walter Reed Hospital that day, but that was his last performance with his sisters.

Various embassies in Washington, DC took turns sending groups to entertain the wounded veterans at Walter Reed Veterans Hospital. At that time, there were still no children among the Embassy families who were trained in Turkish folk dancing, or who had Turkish costumes, so my children were called upon to perform on Turkish holidays.

This hospital performance would prove to be a totally different and surprising experience for Kâmuran and Melike. The Turkish Embassy spokeswoman had decided that, in addition to watching children folk dancing, it would be a special cultural experience for the recuperating veterans to have a taste of famous Turkish coffee, served by Kâmuran and Melike dressed in their pretty costumes. She escorted us down into a large hall on a lower level where small groups of men stood around in pajamas and slippers, or were seated in wheelchairs or straight-backed chairs.

In one corner, a small group of Turkish women (volunteers from the Embassy) were discussing arrangements for preparing the coffee in a traditional, long-handled coffee pot. Each cup had to be cooked slowly over an electric or gas ring in the nearby kitchen, poured with some foam on the top, and served individually while still hot.

Although they were speaking softly in Turkish, I overheard the women murmuring, "... serve each soldier in a wheel chair first."

Standing off to one side, Kâmuran and Melike had missed the instructions in Turkish, and were waiting politely for someone to come and tell them what to do. Before I realized that my girls were totally in the dark about serving the coffee, one of the Turkish ladies brought out the first cup of steaming coffee on a small brass tray, and gave the tray to Kâmuran. It was clear she assumed that the child would pick up the tray with the cup of coffee, carry it over to a soldier in a wheelchair, and gracefully present the cup to him. It was soon clear to *me* that it was *not* clear to Kâmuran, but there were too many chairs between us for me to rush to her side very quickly, and I was too far away to whisper, or to catch her attention. I simply stood immobile, and watched the expressions pass over Kâmuran's face as she looked for instructions from the Turkish women standing nearby, and looked for encouraging directions from the seated soldiers — who were staring in silent fascination. Without losing her calm poise, Kâmuran gave a polite little bow of her head, said *"Tesekkür ederim"* (thank you), picked up the cup of coffee, and drank it!

Now, if Kâmuran were demonstrating how *not* to drink a cup of Turkish coffee, this would have been OK, but to drink it properly, she should have sipped it slowly, one tiny sip at a time, because all the Turkish coffee grounds sink to the bottom, and it is difficult — if not impossible — to *drink* Turkish coffee grounds.

Also, in this situation, Kâmuran's drinking that cup of coffee was totally unacceptable for several other important reasons:

1. Veterans in wheelchairs — the guests of honor, in this case — are *always* served first.

2. Children Kâmuran's age are *never* served before adults — *especially* if there are guests of honor present.

3. Even more importantly, children *never ever* drink this kind of very strong coffee!

A photographer meandering about the room happened to catch the face of the young soldier watching Kâmuran as she lifted the cup. The soldier must have realized that the cup was intended for him, and that the young girl didn't know what to do with it, so she simply drank it — with amazing poise! The young veteran was obviously both fascinated and amused.

After Kâmuran drank that cup of Turkish coffee, she instantly realized her mistake. Then she calmly waited until someone brought her another cup on the tray. Melike, meanwhile, had been watching her sister and sized up the protocol. Overcoming her shyness, she served the next cup, and was ready to answer the soldiers' questions:

"My name is Meh - lee- keh. I was born in Turkey!"

Turkish Dancers at Walter Reed Hospital:
Timur, Kâmuran and Melike Malkoç

EPILOGUE *Before Mrs. Esenbel, the wife of the Turkish Ambassador, left Washington DC (around 1966) she sent me a letter of honorary membership in the Turkish Women's Guild, an honor I have treasured these many decades.*

8

The SQUEAKY DOOR
Poznan, Poland   c 1973

PROLOGUE *This story takes place after I had earned an MA in linguistics, and spent two years on a Fulbright grant teaching English conversation to Polish students in the Adam Mickiewicz University in Poznan, Poland. It was some 15 years or so before the Berlin Wall was torn down, and the Cold War was still casting its pall over the land.*

The Soviets (Russian Communists then in power in Poland) had observation posts everywhere in areas that housed, or were in contact with, foreigners from the West. Most particularly, these were personnel in American embassies in Poland, East Germany, other Soviet-controlled countries in Eastern Europe, and of course, the countries then in the United Soviet Socialist Republic (USSR). All were under continual scrutiny of one kind or another.

In Poland, for instance, I noted that the militia overtly patrolled the streets. Covertly, secret police monitored the comings and goings of "suspicious" persons. Highly trained linguists monitored private telephone calls, letters, telegrams, cables, and other "suspect" communications. Technicians implanted various listening devices in embassies and in private residences.

I saw an obvious example of "eavesdropping implantations" the day I went to pay a courtesy call on the new American professor of linguistics in Poznan, who had arrived with his wife and small daughter that afternoon. He told me this story a few hours later, as he walked me through the apartment.

Their train had arrived on time at the Poznan train station, and the professor and his family were met by their assigned "shepherd" from the Adam Mickiewicz University. They were brought directly from the station by taxi to their assigned apartment.

Apparently the trio had arrived more quickly than expected; another university official had to ask them to wait "while the cleaning crew finished tidying up their freshly-painted apartment." Finally, after a lengthy wait, a second official arrived with a door key, declared that the place was "clean," and ushered the family inside.

It was obvious that not only the paint, but the rough plaster in the center of the middle wall in the living room was still damp. This small detail might well have passed unnoticed, except for one utterly bizarre coincidence: the couple's small daughter, born with an arm deformity and a severe hearing loss, had to wear a finely tuned hearing aid. Whenever the delicate child passed by the area of the re-plastered wall, the freshly installed listening device there set off her hearing aid. It activated a high-pitched sound in her ear, causing her such acute discomfort that the officials were forced to find another apartment for the family immediately — at great upheaval and discomfort to some other residents, I imagine.

Such was the tenor of the times during the Cold War, also referred to by many as "Life behind the Iron Curtain." In any case, life in Poland was never predictable. "Nothing is ever a coincidence here," as my pessimistic Polish colleagues used to remind me.

O ur heroine in the following story — we'll call her Wanda — was an American of Polish ancestry. I assumed this was the reason she had applied to the U.S. Department of Defense School system, specifically seeking a teaching position in Poland. When I met Wanda in the early 1970's, she was assigned to teach school classes in the American Consulate in Poznan, where several Consulate officers had young children of school age.

At the time, I was in my second year of teaching English at Poznan University and my daughter Melike *(pronounced meh' - lee – keh)* was living with me. Because the enrollment in Miss Wanda's classes had dropped to a handful, it had been decided there was room for Melike in the schoolroom in the old consulate building (although strictly speaking, we were not an "American Embassy/Consulate" family).

So it was that Melike had the privilege of attending Miss Wanda's classes for that year, and I had the pleasure of getting to know Wanda myself. I remember first of all, being impressed by her direct approach to life. I remember thinking what a joy it must be to attend her classes. I could see how she must stimulate the children's intellectual curiosity; just making small talk with her during our rare encounters was a pleasure. I always found her perspectives on current situations refreshingly candid, and provocative food for thought.

As the months wore on, I met Wanda on a few more occasions, and then my second year of the Fulbright grant neared an end. My two older daughters, Hikmet and Kâmuran, came to visit for the summer, while I taught classes in a summer course for teachers and English linguistics students.

I'd already made plans to return to the States together with my children when I received a request from the U.S. State Department asking if I would teach a nine-month pilot course — specifically, a refresher course for Polish high school English teachers in the city of Lodz. *(Pronounced woodjz, and located south-west of Warsaw, it was the second or third largest city in Poland at the time.)* For me, this

State Department offer seemed especially promising. I first talked it over with my children, and made arrangements for them to attend school in Seattle the coming year. I saw them off at the airport, and took the train to Lodz.

One might describe a pilot project as a voyage through uncharted waters: it's difficult to predict the outcome. But I was extremely optimistic about the experience I would gain, and hopeful that it would lead to advancement in my teaching career. The Polish Ministry of Education had welcomed this new training program for their English teachers, as English was fast establishing itself as the second language of the world. Not only that, *American* English was rivaling *British* English as an essential tool to multi-lingual international communication. American English was coming into its own, most particularly for science and technology students who aspired to study in the U.S.

Ironically, the Polish officials in the Ministry of Education drew the line at any after-class communication between the pilot course participants (a dozen or more Polish teachers of English) and myself. We rarely met outside my classes, and only at approved functions, where the appointed group monitor was obliged to report all conversations to the government's Communist Party official in charge.

I had been told this was regular Polish Communist Party procedure. I had been briefed before ever setting foot in Poland that politics and religion were two topics to avoid in conversations. What I hadn't expected, though, was that a Party official in Lodz would actually go into the apartment building where I'd been assigned a small flat, and warn the other residents about speaking to me.

I decided not to take it personally, and soon got settled in with my books and few belongings. I studied the train schedules between Lodz and Warsaw, and made myself a daily routine to follow.

Once a week I would take the downtown streetcar to the Lodz train station and then board the morning train for Warsaw. Arriving there, I'd take a streetcar to go to the American Embassy, where I could photocopy my weekly lesson plans and make multiple copies of each course lesson I'd typed out on my portable typewriter. (I was required to submit one copy to the Course Overseer in Lodz for approval, before I could distribute copies to the course participants.)

On each trip to the American Embassy, I would return or pick up an 8mm educational film (also to be shown to the Course Overseer in Lodz for approval). Then I'd enjoy a simple lunch in the Embassy cafeteria, discuss my program with the current English Teaching

Officer who served as my mentor, and chat a bit with Pani Romana, the librarian, before taking a streetcar back to the train station for my return trip to Lodz.

Except for these weekly supply trips to Warsaw, and my long teaching sessions two afternoons each week in Lodz, not a living soul spoke to me. Conversely, I never spoke to a living soul — neither in my apartment building, nor to anyone else. I sometimes wondered if my vocal chords would atrophy from disuse. I dearly missed living in Poznan, where I'd taught for two years under far less restrictive circumstances.

One day, purely by chance, I happened to re-connect with Wanda, and she kindly invited me to visit her in Poznan on one of my lonely train trips. Like her, I'd made so many trips on trains in Poland that the procedure had become less and less of a challenge; in fact, train travel became downright commonplace for me. Perhaps that's why so many details escape my memory.

What I mainly remember of my few visits to Wanda's is that I was always absolutely overjoyed to see her; she was a gloriously hospitable hostess. And I vividly remember her telling me this story of the "Squeaky Door."

Wanda lived on the floor above her classroom in the antique greystone building of Prussian-architectural design, a remnant of an older era in Polish history. The several other large apartments in the building, with its thick concrete walls and massive stone staircases, housed the American Consulate on the street floor, and the consular officers on the next floor up: mostly married couples, whose children attended Wanda's classes in her one-room classroom.

To escape encroaching boredom, and for an occasional bit of excitement outside her classroom, Wanda told me, she would often drop a line to her American friends in West Berlin, setting a weekend date to go shopping in the U.S. Military Post Exchange on the Army base there, and then treat themselves to a special dinner. Wanda's teaching colleagues (I assumed them to be young women roughly her own age, American, and single) loved to haunt the shops and bookstores in the Western sector. They knew their way around the city very well.

One Thursday afternoon not many weeks prior to this story, Wanda bought a round-trip train ticket to West Berlin for the next day. She had planned to spend the weekend with a colleague in West Berlin, "just to shop and relax over a nice dinner." Early that Friday morning, however, she received word from her friend that "something had come up." With many apologies, the friend was postponing the weekend plans until the following weekend.

Wanda was disappointed, but decided to check homework papers and finish lesson plans for the next week, then have a bite of supper and go to bed early for a change. Which she did, first going through her usual evening ritual of drawing the heavy curtains, closing the windows, turning off the lights, and, finally, closing the massive oak door of the apartment.

Only that morning, she recalled happily, she'd finally taken a few minutes to oil the rusting old door hinges. Their squeaking had gotten on her nerves, to the point she thought she'd scream at the sound; she'd even gotten into the habit of opening the door just enough to barely slide through, to minimize the squeaking. So she gave the ancient hinges an extra squirt, and polished the carved surface of the wooden door with furniture polish for good measure. It really was a handsome door, she had to admit, and solid like the rest of the apartment building. It was heavy and built to last.

That evening, alone in her apartment on the top floor, Wanda relaxed in her quiet zone. No sounds from below were ever audible through the thick walls: no sounds from the children below, or from the adults. No rumbles from passing vehicles in the streets. No night owls hooting in the poplar trees.

She did hear rain on the windowpanes, whenever there was a heavy rainstorm. She loved to listen to the rain. Now and then, she heard vague mice-like sounds in the deserted attic above her, but these, too, like the rain, were all *natural* sounds. Otherwise, there was total, utter quietude. In her exhausted state, she found this soothing and relaxing.

She crawled into her four-poster bed that had been pushed into the far corner of the room. This bed was also relaxing. Now, as she tugged the eiderdown quilt over herself, she welcomed the comfort of its gentle warmth. *No wonder it's called a comforter,* she thought, snuggling down and pulling the bed covers completely over her head. She was soon fast asleep.

In the middle of the night, some slight sound woke her from her deep sleep. Wide-awake now and trying to identify the sound, she lay without moving a muscle, except to lift a tiny corner of the eiderdown quilt. She listened for the sound again. *Did I leave the radio on? Or am*

I having a nightmare? Let me analyze the situation, she said to herself, afraid to move an inch.

Her bedroom was totally dark. She analyzed the situation scientifically: *There's no light glowing on the radio, so I know it's not on. I'm not having a nightmare: I just pinched myself, and I felt it.*

It sounds like voices, but it can't be human voices, because no one can get into this apartment without a key. Or, if someone picked the lock and tried to open the door, I would certainly hear that. That squeaky old door makes enough noise to wake the dead!

At this thought, an icy cold flashback shocked her awake instantly, with all her senses alert: *I oiled the hinges this morning, and the door doesn't squeak anymore!*

By now, she began to make out the soft sounds, and to definitely identify them as human voices: Two men's voices, speaking Polish in her living room, to be precise. They were moving slowly now from the living room into her bedroom. *They must be searching through my things! And they're talking to each other! Apparently they're not worried about being overheard in this apartment!*

Another cold realization hit her next: *They must think I took the morning train to Berlin!* She remained motionless under her quilt, with one corner still over her head. She scarcely dared breathe. She heard her desk drawer being pulled out slowly, and things being moved about. Some minutes later, she heard the drawer being shoved back roughly. *They must each have a flashlight and be moving in different directions,* she reasoned. She heard the lock on her briefcase snap open, then a few minutes later, snap shut. Likewise, her dresser drawers were pulled open, and then slammed shut.

She recognized the sound of the metal medicine cabinet in the bathroom being opened and closed, then the sounds of the wooden kitchen cabinets, and the heavy refrigerator door.

Cold chills began creeping over her. When she realized her teeth were about to chatter, she bit down on her tongue, forcing herself, *willing* herself to breathe slowly and silently. Minutes seemed to pass into an eternity.

The last sound she thought she heard was from the desk drawer in the living room, some time ago. This presented the next terrifying conundrum: *How will I know when they've really gone?*

In the silence of her room, in the warmth of the eiderdown quilt still covering her from head to foot, she decided to force herself to relax, so she could fall asleep again. She knew she was strong-willed enough to do this. What else could she do?

Eventually, she did fall asleep for some hours, apparently. This time when she awoke, she could tell it was early morning because her bedroom was no longer pitch black: a pale sliver of daylight came through the edge of the curtains.

She pulled a corner of the feather comforter away from her head, so she could see the poplar tree near the window, and a bird on an overhanging branch. The normalcy of it all slowly eased her back to her familiar surroundings. The events of the night now seemed like a mere nightmare.

EPILOGUE *Had it been a nightmare? In the morning light, she could find no signs of disturbance anywhere, nothing missing or out of place, no evidence of any kind to show that intruders had ever been there.*

No one called to check on the train trip to West Berlin that she had cancelled. No one seemed to even know she had cancelled it; no one called about her weekend. The downstairs neighbors had not commented on any midnight noises in the building. Nothing unusual was reported at all. . . .

That was the end of Wanda's story, as I recall her telling of it, how many decades ago. Since then, I had moved on, entered the Foreign Service at the age of 50 and served 15 years, mainly in Turkey, Poland, and Washington DC. Now, I'm twice retired.

I once looked up Wanda somewhere on the East Coast, I can't recall when exactly. She had retired from teaching, and was involved in quite a different career: managing a jazz band, I think she said. She told me she'd lost a lot of weight, felt wonderful, and loved her new vocation. I remember writing down her address on a small slip of paper and putting it on the little telephone shelf.

Shortly thereafter, I reached mandatory retirement age, moved back to my home in Spokane, Washington, and then to the Seattle area to be near my four children and three grandsons. By the time I had resettled after the second move and was able to resume correspondence, I found I had left the telephone shelf with the small slip of paper behind, and so I lost all track of Wanda. She might be in her sixties now, as I am already halfway through my eighties.

Before writing this story, I looked up a Foreign Service acquaintance I'd known in Poznan, who told me that the historic Consulate building had finally been razed to the ground. In the demolition process, the workmen reported finding small rooms honeycombing the rear of the attic, with extensive wiring to the entire building, and some kind of alternate exit in the back.

I made several searches on the Internet for Wanda's real name in the directories, but apparently her combination of Polish names is as common as Mary Smith or Jane Doe is in English: dozens of Barbara Sapas popped up with addresses in Poland and in the U.S. It was an impossible task for me, I regret to say.

I wanted so much to talk with her, to fill in some blanks, and to ask her permission to tell this story. I wanted to tell her how much I admired her bright and creative intellect. I wanted to thank her once again for all her kind and generous hospitality at a time when often I had absolutely no human being to talk to.

Will our paths cross once again? I keep hoping.

9

The BULGARIAN BUG
Sofia, Bulgaria 1984

PROLOGUE   In the summer of 1984, two of my daughters, Hikmet and Kâmuran, had come to visit me in Warsaw. Our grand plan was for Kâmuran (the only one of us who had an international driver's license) to drive my new Volvo to Istanbul. She would drop me off so I could spend a month's home leave with my late husband's family and friends in Turkey, while she and sister Hikmet traveled around to interesting archeological sites in regions they'd never had a chance to visit when they were growing up.

Now, armed with maps of Eastern Europe, travel advisories from the American Embassy in Warsaw, confirmed hotel reservations in Budapest and Sofia, and a full tank of gas, we three set out in high spirits and happy hearts.

O ur itinerary took us south, through the medieval city of Krakow, the "cultural gem of Poland," on through the corner of *(then)* Czechoslovakia to Hungary's capital city of Budapest.

An Embassy friend had helped make reservations for our stop there: "One room for three — my two daughters and myself — for one night at a four-star hotel." Somehow, by the time we arrived in Budapest, the multi-lingual message had been garbled into "three rooms for one night at a four-star hotel."

I held my tongue about the expensive error, thinking that perhaps I should take a look first, before asking the hotel to rectify the mistake. Kâmuran, who'd been driving all day, and Hikmet, who as navigator had been interpreting road maps and signs for her, were both so tired. I knew they would appreciate the luxury of private rooms, and a really good night's sleep. So, I thanked the bellhop, and was escorted into my single room, small and well appointed. Hardly rating four stars, I thought, until I stepped out onto the tiny wrought-iron balcony. From this vantage point, I found myself overlooking the storied Danube River!

To dramatize this historical view that lay almost directly across from our hotel, floodlights had been artistically positioned on the riverbank to shroud the bend of the river in velvety blackness, while casting a golden light high above the fairy-tale spires and turrets of the medieval castle dominating the scene.

Then, as if Mother Nature needed to top off that breathtaking panorama, a dramatically silvery-white moon added its fabulous splendor, shining down upon the romantic panorama below, catching here and there a silver glint of the rippling river. I was quite swept away at the sight. After dinner, Kâmuran, Hikmet, and I each settled into our single rooms, then sat outside, nearly elbow to elbow on our tiny private balconies, conversing softly in the summer air, and glorying in the magical night scene.

We slumbered deeply and sweetly throughout the night, dreaming of the moonlit Danube. In the morning, we showered and dressed at our leisure.

Wonderfully refreshed, we each stepped out upon our tiny private balconies to enjoy a continental breakfast with freshly brewed coffee, chitchatting back and forth across the railings, and reveling in the bright morning sunshine.

After breakfast, though, it was suddenly back to reality: packing up, checking out of the charming hotel, and merging into the transcontinental traffic heading eastward.

Our travel guides had suggested we route ourselves through Belgrade, Yugoslavia and continue on to Bulgaria. The American Embassy guides had strongly advised us to avoid Rumania, stressing that though both were Communist-block countries "behind the Iron Curtain" at the time, of the two choices Bulgaria was "much preferable."

At their suggestion, I had reserved a hotel room south of Belgrade, in the Bulgarian capital of Sofia. This was to be our next stop after romantic Budapest, and only a day's drive to Turkey. I knew we'd probably have a hard time finding any other hotel to admit us Westerners during that era, and I tried to be carefully specific in making the reservation: one room, with three beds — or one double bed and a single.

Altogether, it had been a long day's drive from Bucharest to Sofia, and night had fallen by the time Kâmuran pulled into the hotel's underground parking area.

My first impression upon entering the hotel lobby was not just the newness, but also the enormity of the building, designed perhaps for huge international conferences. There were few other tourists in sight, however.

The floors of the lobby were glistening with large tiles of brown marble; at the lobby corners, vertical columns several stories high were covered with large squares of contrasting white marble. From the vast overhead space above hung elaborate crystal chandeliers, their elongated prisms glittering and shimmering as they reflected the lobby lights. Bordering the lobby area on one side was an open staircase that descended from the floor above; the lobby itself was decorated with tall potted palmettos, and generously furnished with oversized brown leather sofas and chairs clustered invitingly in conversational groups.

At the reception desk, a polite clerk speaking excellent English checked us in and collected our passports "to be retained until departure." He also collected $125 U.S. for our triple-occupancy one-night room. I suppressed a gasp, and bit my tongue. Perhaps this would also turn out to be a fabulous four-star hotel, such as we had just experienced in Budapest.

Another polite young employee came to stack our bags onto a cart, indicating that we should follow him in the elevator to an upper floor. As we trailed behind him silently, I noted the sparseness of décor in the long corridors, in striking contrast to the ornate lobby.

The elevator doors opened on the third floor, directly across from the third-floor attendant's station. The heavyset woman with impassive face but alert eyes sat positioned in such a way behind her desk that she could see the comings and goings of every hotel guest and employee on that floor. I smiled and nodded to her as we passed, murmuring a greeting in Polish that I hoped sounded Slavic enough to be taken as a friendly salutation.

Switching quietly into Turkish to speak with my daughters, I delicately reminded them that we were so-called "Western Capitalists," hence we were "suspect" in this Communist country. Everything and everyone here may be monitored. More so than the monitoring in Poland, I emphasized. They nodded a bit impatiently as if to say: How many times do you have to remind us, Mother? You know we're always polite!

The well-trained bellhop opened our door, deposited our bags, and departed smoothly. Kâmuran, always meticulous about matters of health and cleanliness, immediately went in to check out the tiny bathroom, while Hikmet stood in the center of the small room, trying to visualize how the wooden settee against one wall could unfold into a double bed, and who would sleep on the single-width wooden settee against the other wall. With the little table and two chairs, there was scarcely space left over for our bags, which we didn't want to leave in the car.

At this point, Kâmuran suddenly let out an agonized screech. She had just opened the door of the tiny bathroom, barely large enough to hold the small bathtub, and was pointing inside: *"Eeek! There's an insect!"*

Hikmet rushed to Kâmuran's side to take a peek, while I tried to calm her down by pointing frantically to the bright copper light fixture hanging from the center of the ceiling in our room. I made wild hand gestures signaling her to *shut up*. But she didn't. Responding in agitated English, she said, "Mother, don't tell me to hush! This tub is *not clean!* How can we take a shower in *here?"*

I knew she was terribly tired from driving, and was now annoyed that she couldn't take a shower, so I tried to mollify her: "Sweetheart, we can wash in the wash basin in the toilet room. See, here's the little toilet room, right next to the bath room. Look! I have a whole bottle of lemon cologne. We always used that cologne as a disinfectant in Turkey, do you remember? I just love the fresh scent, don't you?"

I was babbling on in a desperate effort to calm her, and get her to *stop talking*. It was only a few minutes later, it seemed, when a sharp knock on the door stopped all of us from talking. *What now?* I wondered with a little shiver, as I automatically opened the door. Standing stock still in the doorway were two figures straight out of science fiction. First was the impassive third-floor matron, repeating something in Bulgarian that sounded like an official edict of tremendous import.

The second figure was the polite young man who'd brought us our baggage, now standing in stiff attention at the matron's side, repeating a word that sounded like *"disinfectant."* He was wearing dark-red rubber gloves, a facemask, and holding some kind of bag contraption with a long, plastic-hose attachment over his shoulder. My immediate impression was: *"He's got bagpipes! No, it can't be bagpipes! He's not a Scot!"* I had a wild urge to giggle.

I caught my breath and gasped, "Oh, please come in!" I nodded to the pair, while pulling the door wide open so the girls and I could first step out into the corridor — and give the strange pair space enough to squeeze into the small room. The "disinfector" marched straight into the bathroom and prepared to aim his plastic hose at the bathtub; the matron quickly closed the bathroom door behind him. Kâmuran's jaw had dropped and she was now speechless.

From out in the corridor, we could hear the plastic hose going *Swish! Swish!* inside the tiny room. Then, after an extra *Swish! Swish!* for good measure, the young man exited the bathroom, shut that door, and followed the floor matron out into the hall. She closed the door of the room behind them, and they rushed off. I hurried after, to say *"Thank you"* in as many languages as I could muster, although that was really the last thing in the world I wanted to say to them.

The girls and I re-entered our tiny room, immediately snatching up towels to cover our noses. Hikmet and Kâmuran tried valiantly to open the narrow window, to no avail. It was hermetically sealed.

I could never mistake the smell of DDT. It brought back memories of our ten years in the oilfields of southeastern Turkey where my late husband had been a petroleum engineer. I remembered how the terribly toxic disinfectant DDT was used to eradicate endemic fleas that thrived on the earthen floors in the villagers' adobe houses. DDT also eradicated the flies and mosquitoes in public places (including the small movie house that showed weekly films for our enjoyment). That was all several decades ago, before the Turkish Ministry of Health outlawed DDT. Apparently, it hadn't been outlawed as yet in Bulgaria.

We three snatched up our purses and wallets and fled from the noxious fumes in the room. For a little exercise, and to clear our lungs, we took the stairs down instead of the elevator. Breathing freely, we descended in leisurely fashion to the spacious restaurant on the main floor.

Only a handful of other tourists were seated for dinner; I presumed this was because it was nearing the end of the summer season. An attentive *maitre d'* appeared with elaborate menus listing page after page of mouth-watering appetizers, soups, entrees, beverages, and desserts. Each item was written in elegant script in Bulgarian, Russian, German, Italian, and English.

We pored over each page, discussing what our selections would be, getting hungrier and hungrier. Vegetarian Kâmuran took an extra long time looking for her favorite vegetables and other non-meat dishes on the menu. When the *maitre d'* returned to take our orders, we were ready with our selection, but one by one, the polite young man shook his head at our choices. "No, sorry," was his only comment, with a polite, but resigned, expression. Once, I thought I heard a little sigh escape his lips.

"Oh," said Hikmet politely, as the light dawned. "What do you have on the menu *this evening?*"

The headwaiter quickly pointed to a few (mainly pork) entrees, and waited for our revised selection. So much for the pages of fancy menu listings!

Ironically, we were in no hurry at all to return to our room, and eventually a waiter brought our food. The three of us chatted while we chewed slowly, savoring the cheese appetizers. We nibbled the pork entrees and root vegetables slowly and thoughtfully. We lingered long over the dessert of bread-pudding, reminiscing and laughing softly at happy shared memories. We ordered after-dinner demitasses, drinking the strong black coffee one sip at a time, discussing our itinerary and post-arrival plans in Turkey.

By now, we had frittered away as much time as we possibly could at the dinner table. So, unanimously, we agreed to return to our room, somehow get through the night, and leave as early as possible in the morning. In our suitcases, we found enough silk scarves to wrap around our heads and noses to mask the toxic fumes in the room, then pulled the bed sheets as far up as they would go over our heads. We managed, however fitfully, to sleep through the night.

By first light the next morning, we were already up and dressed and had carried our bags down to the lobby. It was still so early there was no one in sight in the lobby except the all-night reception clerk. I paid the bill without a murmur, and we three rushed down to the parking lot with our bags.

When Kâmuran opened the trunk to stow the bags, she remarked quietly that someone had evidently tried to force open the trunk lock, but nothing seemed to be missing. I decided not to put in a complaint at the front desk, preferring to leave as quickly as possible.

We couldn't depart that hotel soon enough to suit me. Once we were clear of the hotel garage, we opened all the car windows, inhaled great gulps of clean air, and wished each other good luck as we set out on the open road.

"I'm hungry!" were the first words from our dear driver. I quickly offered her crackers and fruit juice from the snack bag. But what she really wanted, she declared, was *coffee*; it helped her to feel awake and alert for the road. "I have to look for a coffee shop!"

"Where do you think you are, Sweetheart?" I asked her. "In this country, there's no place like that open this time of the morning!"

Unconvinced, she slowed down at the end of the street, where it joined the main highway. "Look! See that sign down the side street there? It says *Café!*"

"We have to stay on the highway, Sweetheart," I reminded her, again in vain. She was already turning off the main street toward the side street. Within the blink of an eye, two men wearing police uniforms and waving little round lollypops on sticks, jumped out from behind a clump of bushes on the street corner.

They were shouting, *"Transit! Transit!"* and their warning was unmistakable. We were *not* permitted to stray from the international highway. Like the restaurant menus, the sign on the corner was printed elegantly in the same five languages: Bulgarian, Russian, German, Italian, and English. Even from my limited view from the back seat, it had been clearly visible on the right side of the road. So much for Kâmuran's quest for coffee at the café!

The next several hours passed tediously as we drove along the monotonous highway that cut arrow-straight through the flat and empty countryside. Only rarely did I see any villages in the far-off distance to the left or right of our transit highway; there were no connecting roads to be seen at all. At last, Kâmuran slowed down when she spotted the road sign: **Rest Stop ahead: Restrooms, Water, Gas, Beverages, Food.** Also the usual five-language sign warning: **Do not stray from the International Highway.**

We made a beeline first for the restrooms, then headed for the café. I'd spotted a sign advertising **Gift Shop**, and had to explore for a souvenir of this memorable journey. It took me some time, and I finally settled on a **"Wood Carving, Typical Bulgarian Floral Motif."** I'd already paid for it when I saw, too late, the tiny chip of white plaster-of-Paris where the brown paint had flaked off. Still, I decided the non-wood carving *was* a souvenir, and I carried it off to the café to show the girls.

Inside, I met with another shock, but a most pleasant one this time: It was Hikmet and Kâmuran, perched on stools at the counter, hobnobbing with the café chef and his assistants! They were all nodding and smiling and laughing. Like they were old friends; like they were kinfolk! And they were speaking Turkish! For my daughters, it was such a relief to be able to understand and *speak* to strangers, especially strangers who were friendly and smiling. As Hikmet said, "They're *not* strangers, Mother! They're *Turks!*"

The two would have been so happy to linger at that roadside café all morning, but the highway beckoned, and we still had many miles to cover before our final destination that evening. From the warm and welcoming café of the Bulgarian Turks, we traveled on through Plodov near the Bulgarian border, and had no problems crossing into Turkey at the dusty border town of Edirne, the ancient Greek city of Adrianopolis. There, the Turkish border guards took note of the Volvo on my passport, checked the car's papers and all our passports, then welcomed us into Turkey: *"Hos geldininz!"*

In unison, we three responded to his traditional welcome: *"Hos bulduk!"* With lightened hearts, we headed south toward our destination: the little town of Küçükçekmece ("a small cove") on the Strait of Bosphorus — one of the many outlying suburbs on the European side of the sprawling metropolis of Istanbul.

EPILOGUE   *I had written ahead to my elder sister-in-law, Sulhiye, with an approximate date of our arrival. I knew she and her daughters had been stuffing grape leaves with rice; stuffing bell peppers with minced lamb; rolling cheese pastries with parsley; steaming rice pilav with pine nuts; baking eggplant in tomato, garlic and olive oil; seasoning rice pudding with nutmeg; and chopping walnut meats for honeyed baklava, all in preparation for our welcome dinner.*

At the sound of our car rolling up in front of the vine-covered stucco house, the front lights turned on all at once. Now we could see the old fig tree in the corner of the front garden, the walkway to the wrought-iron gate, and the steps up to the front door.

When the door suddenly burst open, we found ourselves lovingly embraced by aunts, uncles, cousins, nephews, and nieces. There were hugs and kisses, and hands reaching out to carry our bags into the house. Although we were 7,000 miles from America, we felt the comforting warmth of home. It was like turning the family clock back to Long Ago.

10

***The* LONELY WOMAN *in the*
TURKISH CUSTOMS HOUSE**
Istanbul, Turkey 1984

The Galata Bridge, pictured on the right, leads to the Old Customs House in Istanbul. Painting by Derman Över.

PROLOGUE *At some time or other, everyone in my husband's large family in Turkey called on our nephew Ercan [pronounced air-john] for favors. By nature, he is generous-hearted and always willing to help anyone with any problems. Now, it seemed, it was my turn to ask him for a favor. A large favor.*

I explained it as simply as I could: On this visit to Turkey from Poland where I was working in the American Embassy, I had entered Turkey in my new Volvo with my daughters Kâmuran and Hikmet. Kâmuran had an international driving permit, so she did all the driving on this trip. The border guards at the Turkish checkpoint in Edirne checked all our passports, while I sat in the front seat holding the documents showing my ownership of the new car. After examining all the papers, the official entered the Volvo numbers in my passport and waved us on.

During the following month, while I visited my sisters-in-law and former teaching colleagues, Hikmet and Kâmuran had a merry time visiting famous archeological sites, also all their relatives who lived near those regions. Now, during the last week of my vacation, the two girls had driven back to meet me in Istanbul. I promised to let them use the car for the rest of the summer, and then drive it back to Warsaw. I would take an earlier plane back to Warsaw.

We three had been visiting Ercan and his family in an outlying suburb of Istanbul near the international airport. As a customs broker, he had a small office near the Customs House.

That morning, Ercan called to say he'd been checking on customs regulations concerning automobiles brought into Turkey, and had sent a message to the Customs Director's office.

The Director's response had been: "Irregular procedure! Who was driving the car on entering the country? Who is the owner? Why doesn't the owner return with the car to where she came from?"

Ercan didn't know how to answer these questions. He feared there might be complications if I tried to leave the country without the car, while the car was still written on my passport. He made an appointment to speak with the Director about my case early the next morning, and suggested I should accompany him.

The Customs House is a warehouse in the historic district of Istanbul — a cavernous, empty building several stories high, with overhead cranes running on tracks out to the water. Here, service boats brought shipments into the Istanbul Port Authorities, to be cleared and off-loaded and moved into the Customs House.

Nephew Ercan and I settled down at a small café table near one of the glassed-in Customs Offices. He ordered tea from the roving tea-and-coffee man, and excused himself to check on messages. As a customs broker, he spent a lot of time walking to and from his small office near the Customs House.

No one except Ercan had come into or out of our side of the warehouse for several hours. When it neared noon, he ordered hot lunch brought from the café next door: meatballs in tomato sauce with rice pilav and a side of green beans. He ate hurriedly, apologized for running off again to check for incoming cables. I assured him that I was only too happy to wait.

From time to time, he returned to check on messages concerning Volvos. I dawdled over my lunch, one small bite at a time, chewing as slowly as I could.

The roving young man with the brass tray brought me a cup of medium-sweet Turkish coffee, ordered by thoughtful Ercan. As I sipped it delicately, I thought of the book I should have brought along to read. I began to study my old pocket map of Istanbul, to see if I could spot my present location, or if I could memorize a few more place names.

Now and then, I would see someone coming in or going out of the other side of the enormous warehouse. Gradually, as my eyes grew accustomed to the dim light, I became aware of an immobile figure seated at a table on the far side, toward the darker end of the building.

In my boredom, I began to study the figure to see, first of all, whether it was a man or a woman. *If that's a man, never mind! He's used to being all alone*, I thought to myself. *But if it's a woman, all alone, perhaps I can help her. I really empathize with lonely women. I've been alone so much in my travels.*

Such were my idle thoughts in my boredom, as I kept my eyes fixed on the seated figure. Even with my near-sightedness, I could gradually make out some details, beginning with the shoes protruding from under the table. These appeared to be small, and rather delicate.

Above, on the top of the head, I could see a bit of a small woolen cap. This was definitely a woman's cap. Her head was bowed, and she seemed to be writing in a book! To me, a writer, that was definitely *a sign!* I waited until Ercan came back to check at the adjacent office, then told him I was going to walk over to talk to that lonely-looking woman. "Perhaps she'd like a Turkish coffee," I said.

"Oh, I'll order one for her, Aunt," said generous-hearted Ercan.

"No, thank you, Ercan. I want to talk to her myself. She looks lonely!" He smiled at me as I waved and set off on the trek across the expanse of concrete floor to the far side, and down the other side of the warehouse. Keeping my eyes fixed on the woman, I took in more details as I walked slowly toward her table: Her coat was light grey, tweedy-looking, her brown leather "sensible" shoes looked well made and suitable for walking. She herself looked to be medium height, of slight build, with light brown or blondish hair.

Then a wild, bizarre thought struck me: *She has a kind of Polish look!* This bizarre thought was followed by another weird thought: *Even her raincoat has a kind of Polish look!*

Have I been working so long in Poland that every light brown-haired woman in a raincoat looks Polish? I wondered. *Oh, no! Poland is in another dimension, totally. Wake up!* I say to myself. *I'm not far, far away — I'm visiting in Turkey! My beloved second home!*

My footsteps automatically slow down as I mentally sort out these wild, weird thoughts. By the time I reach the woman's table, I have come to a complete stop. My vision has cleared, my head has cleared, and I burst out in total astonishment: "Pani Lucyna!"

"Pani Anna Maria!" she responds in equal astonishment.

EPILOGUE *I ordered two Turkish coffees from the roving server, and sat down to catch my breath and recover my equilibrium.*

I had first met Lucyna several years before, when I was teaching in a summer refresher course for Polish teachers of English in Krakow. More recently, we met again in Warsaw, where she was now working as the official Polish translator in the Turkish Embassy there. She was also developing a Polish/Turkish dictionary in her free time, she told me. During her university years, I knew, she'd received degrees in both English and Turkish, and was continuing her active reading in both languages.

I also knew that during that era of the Communist regime in Poland, it was difficult for Poles to get permission to travel abroad except to other Communist countries. However, because she was an officially certified translator, she had been granted permission to attend an international conference on Turkish linguistics held in Ankara. She was fortunate to attend that wonderfully stimulating event, she confided to me, and promised to send me a copy of her dictionary if it ever got published. She gave a little laugh.

I thanked her in advance, but said that didn't explain what she was doing all alone here in the Customs House in Istanbul. No linguistics conference here! I smiled at the thought. She smiled back, shaking her head a little, then explained seriously that she had bought a piece of beautiful Turkish marble for her father's gravestone. She was going to have the precious white marble crated for shipping to Poland, and had been waiting for the export permission papers.

Before our coffee had even cooled, a customs clerk arrived to hand her the export papers. Now she had no time to spare, she said, only for another quick hug. I wished her a happy journey, and gave her a wave for the road.

When I returned to my seat at the first table, Ercan was waiting with a wide smile on his face. "Yenge," (Aunt) he said happily, "I have explained everything to the Director. The car is off your passport, and everything is OK! All you have to do is sign this paper right here, and Kâmuran can drive your car back to Warsaw!"

Later that fall, back in Warsaw, I attended a special exhibit of oil paintings by the Cultural Attaché of the Turkish Embassy. It was a popular charity event, with the sales proceeds going to support Polish children's orphanages. I went to take a look, and to congratulate the Cultural Attaché on his artwork. I deliberated over several brilliant seascapes, and decided they would be great gifts for my family. The artistic attaché thanked me for my donation, and hospitably offered me a cup of Turkish coffee. As we conversed in Turkish, I mentioned having met the Polish translator for their embassy in Warsaw some years ago, at an English-language summer course in Poland.

"Ah, yes, Pani Lucyna," he smiled. "We are all fond of Pani Lucyna. We depend on her so much. In fact, every night I pray for her good health."

The attaché's assistant, overhearing our Turkish conversation, couldn't resist chiming in. "Yes, that's true, Malkoç hanim. We all pray for Pani Lucyna's good health!"

At this, I must have looked surprised at the passionately warm-hearted feelings expressed about such a quiet, hardworking, and modest teacher/translator. How wonderfully kind! It must be another rule in the Moslem religion, I thought to myself. I knew all about helping widows and orphans — this exhibit was a beautiful example of helping orphans — but I wondered which category Pani Lucyna fell into. She was not a widow: I'd met her husband in Warsaw!

The witty attaché soon enlightened me, with a straight face but a twinkle in his eye. "Yes, Malkoç hanim, we all pray for Pani Lucyna, especially in the cold and rainy season. May Allah protect her! Because if Pani Lucyna gets the flu, she has to stay home until she recovers. Meanwhile, all her work as official translator of foreign mail piles up. We don't receive any Embassy mail from Turkey until she has checked it. Indeed, we pray daily for her good health!"

Several years passed after that most interesting visit to the Turkish art exhibit and, according to schedule, I had been transferred from Warsaw to Washington, DC, on my last assignment before retirement.

One day, a small, carefully wrapped parcel arrived in my mailbox: a freshly printed, pocket-sized Polish-Turkish dictionary, the cover printed in fancy gold lettering: Lucyna Antonowicz-Bauer. This was tangible proof that her remarkable diligence and perseverance had finally carried her through to publication.

Her precious dictionary sits in a special place on my bookshelf. On the rare occasions when I have to write something in Polish, I pick it up to check on a word or phrase, and leaf through the pages nostalgically. Then I picture the modest woman with the many linguistic talents sitting alone in the Istanbul Customs House, waiting patiently to ship her father's white marble gravestone to Poland.

May he rest in peace.

11

WRITING *"EASY PLAYS in ENGLISH"*
1985, Istanbul;
1986, Warsaw;
1993, Regents/Prentice Hall, Englewood Cliffs, NJ

PROLOGUE   Foreign Service assignment in Ankara: 1979 - 1983

The idea of writing little plays for the English-language classroom came to me indirectly one day from an experienced Turkish teacher of English. He had first walked into the American Embassy located nearby, looking for English-teaching information, and was sent over to our office in the U.S. Information Service (USIS).

At the time, USIS was an overseas local branch of the U.S. Information Agency (USIA), the agency that had assigned me as English Teaching Officer (ETO). Later, USIA became a part of the U.S. State Department.

To avoid bureaucratic confusion, I found it necessary to keep the latest updated Abbreviations List handy.

I rose to greet my visitor, he introduced himself, and we shook hands. "Good afternoon, Mrs. Malkoç!" he said. (My married name is Turkish, and rhymes with ball - coach.)

"I'm searching for teaching materials for my high-school students," he began. "They want to practice speaking English in conversational situations. Can you help me?"

"I'm sorry, Ahmet bey," I answered him. "I wish I had something like little plays to offer you. We have only grammar exercises and readers."

His departing suggestion was: "Why don't you <u>write</u> some little plays, Mrs. Malkoç?"

"Maybe I will some day," I laughed, as we shook hands and he went on his way.

His idea lingered in my mind, though, because I'd been thinking of doing some creative writing in my free time.

So, the very next weekend, I sat down with my portable typewriter and thought up a simple plot for an unusual conversational situation.

"MARTY the MARTIAN: A Classroom Play for English-Language Learners"

The Scene: A small-town square

Characters: Many different people in the town, and **Marty**

The Situation: Many people are walking around, looking at a strange black box that has dropped from the planet Mars. A voice inside is talking to the people in the street, and asking them questions. . . .

I showed the first copy of this play to my friend Barbara Gülen, director of the English-teaching staff in the Bi-Cultural Turkish-American Center in Ankara; I knew Barbara had trained in theater arts in college. After reading the play, she asked to try it out with the intermediate-level evening students at the Center.

*Several months later, Barbara called to report great success with **"Marty the Martian."** The students had worked diligently on their roles, had constructed some simple stage props and a cardboard box for **Marty**. When they were ready, she put up posters announcing the forthcoming evening performance in the auditorium. Later, she reported that a large number of the students' families had attended, and had applauded enthusiastically.*

I was quite encouraged, so much so, in fact, that I mentioned the little play to an enterprising English teacher in Istanbul. He was establishing a new bookshop that would feature English-language books. "If you write a book of plays, Mrs. Malkoç, I'll publish it!"

"If I write a book of plays, Önder bey, I'll send you the manuscript!" I promised. Not long after that, my four-year assignment in Turkey came to a close, and I went off to a similar teacher-training assignment in Poland.

It took some weeks before I felt settled enough into my new situation and my new responsibilities to even think about free weekend activities, and really quite a long while before I decided to commit my free weekends to creative writing.

Eventually, it was because of this commitment to creative writing that I found myself in situations I would never have dreamed of, even in my wildest scenarios.

But first, a bit of background behind this decision, and the subsequent twists of fate that led me to surprising — and sometimes bittersweet — successes.

Flash-back to Poznan, Poland: academic years 1970 - 1972

To my delight, I was given a two-year grant from the State Department/Fulbright Commission/U.S. Information Agency to teach English at Adam Mickiewicz University in the city of Poznan.

This was an exciting teaching/learning experience, one that enriched and furthered my career. At the same time, it broadened horizons for my teen-age children in Boxhill Boarding School in Sussex, England. On their long school holidays, and during the summers, they took turns flying to visit their many aunts, uncles, and cousins in Turkey; alternately, they took a train to visit me in Poland.

Flash-back to Lodz, Poland: academic year 1973 *The USIA office asked me to set up an experimental refresher course for Polish secondary-school English-language teachers in the city of Lodz. [pronounced woojdz]*

Again, I felt enriched professionally by this experience of planning and implementing twice-weekly programs, and preparing teaching materials appropriate for these high-school teachers. At the same time, I had a different kind of experience that was not altogether surprising, but still unforgettable. This was the shock of being quietly shunned.

Not only had the Polish teachers been advised by their directors to limit their contact with me strictly to the classroom; the residents adjacent to my unit in the Lodz apartment building had been individually warned by the security police to avoid me. As an American sponsored by the American Embassy, I was considered "suspect."

My schedule included the two days a week I had sessions with the teachers, and the weekly train trip up to the American Embassy in Warsaw where I made copies of my lesson materials on the ditto machine, and picked up short educational films in English that were suitable for discussion topics. I spent the rest of my days in my apartment making lesson plans; in effect, I was writing my own methodology book.

Without a telephone, I never spoke to a soul while I was in my apartment, of course. I did speak to clerks in the separate little shops in the neighborhood where I sallied out to buy bread, groceries, and milk. Sometimes I ordered a hot dish at the corner Milk Bar, which was a kind of simple cafeteria — but my Polish vocabulary was limited mainly to basic phrases and polite expressions.

In retrospect, I realize now that on some days I never actually opened my mouth to speak at all. I told myself not to take this shunning personally: it was simply a condition of being an American living behind "the Iron Curtain" during "the Cold War."

Otherwise, apart from the shunning and the surveillance, my life was simple and relatively uneventful. Always most important in my assignment in Poland was learning to recognize and respect the delicate politics involved, and to appreciate the patient efforts of the many Polish and American educators to maintain the fragile bridge of cultural/educational exchange between our two countries.

Despite the depressing restrictions imposed by the Soviets (Russians) in Poland at that time, I found the academic environment tremendously stimulating: the Polish teachers and students whom I met in the classrooms were intelligent, creative, and keen on perfecting their English. It was a pleasure to teach them.

Not all Poles were members of the Communist Party, I should note. During this era, many were involved in the growing Solidarity underground movement to end Soviet control of the Polish government. Until nearly the end of the 1980's, however, the Polish government continued to remain officially Communist. Their officials frowned on, in effect, forbade, doing business with "decadent Western capitalists." Specifically, this meant the Americans in the American Embassy.

At the same time, the Polish government was anxious to send their Polish scientists, physicists, and other high-level personnel to study in the U.S. in order to acquire English-language fluency as well as gain cutting-edge knowledge in their professional fields.

The Polish Ministry of Education was also anxious to continue the intensive English-language seminars for their secondary-school English teachers and their third-year university students of English linguistics. These courses were held every summer, also occasionally during the year, at various sites in Poland. Most of these courses were co-sponsored by the British Council and the USIA, who jointly provided the course directors, instructors, teaching material, and use of equipment at the seminar sites. For eleven summers, I participated in these intensive "immersion" courses. All of these educational efforts were part of the above-mentioned "fragile bridge" of continuing educational exchange.

It seemed like a game of "quid pro quo." By special dispensation of the Polish Ministry of Education, the seminar participants were allowed to receive generous USIA and British Council gifts to support the lectures and language courses: brand-new English grammar books, readers, conversation books, pocket dictionaries, and illustrated booklets of Americana, and life in the British Isles. This was astonishing to me — not the generosity of the gifts, but the fact that the teachers were allowed to keep the gifts. I'd heard that for some years, U.S. publications were not being imported into Poland, and that many Poles with relatives in America wanted to send books and couldn't.

On the other hand, I was told publications from Soviet-bloc countries were imported freely. This ban on English books created hardships for the Polish teachers trying valiantly to teach English, but having nothing to teach from but antiquated methodology books and unbelievably out-dated language books to read ("Uncle Tom's Cabin" for example). Up-to-date copies of British and American texts carried

97

in from the outside were treasured by English teachers. Many precious texts were shared — and sometimes tediously copied out in longhand, page by page.

Once, a Polish teacher let it slip in my presence that language-seminar participants were not allowed to befriend anyone from the American Embassy. I was not surprised. Before arriving in Poznan back in 1970, I had been briefed on the general "Do's and Don'ts in Poland," beginning with the "No-No" topics for discussion: politics and religion.

During a summer course one day, I was invited to sit at the back of the room to observe a colleague's class; we shared ideas for practical teaching techniques this way. Out of the corner of my eye, I happened to notice a stranger slipping in and out of the room every hour or so during the class. "Is he an inspector?" I wondered quietly to the participant next to me.

"No, he's the reporter for this group. He has to report to the Party official on every session. Each group in the seminar has one," she whispered back. Personally, the reporter reminded me of a tattletale schoolboy. But later, I understood that this reporting on classes was a way of life in Poland at that time. I didn't like the idea, but it wasn't any of my business, so I never made comments about it. I simply became inured to the various modes of monitoring and surveillance that were forms of Soviet control.

Flash-forward to Warsaw: Foreign Service Assignment 1983-1987
How well I remember the first day of my ETO assignment in the American Embassy in Warsaw in 1983. How impressed I was by my fellow Americans, how well-trained in their work, and how well-briefed on their restricted boundaries, travel regulations, and curfews. The spick-and-span, physically fit Marine guards on round-the-clock duty especially commanded my respect.

I was also impressed by how smoothly the local Polish staff carried out their various job responsibilities, following the protocol and decorum required to run an embassy.

While I would come to know many of the Americans on a more personal basis, of course, I would learn next to nothing about the Poles outside their Embassy jobs. And I never tried to.

Again, I would learn to adjust to working as an American in the American Embassy, and to living as a foreigner in Poland. More than anything, I was eager to tackle my job responsibilities as set out by the Polish Ministry of Education. Some programs were sponsored by the USIA / State Department with the cooperation of the American

Embassy in Warsaw; about half of the programs were jointly sponsored by the British Council.

I was fortunate to have had a good model to follow from the 1970's: a highly respected and experienced ETO, George McCready. When I'd arrived as an instructor during my first summer, the seminar was held in the famous shrine city of Czêstochova (Chen-sto-hova), where George was co-director with his British Council counterpart. Now, 15 years later, I would be directing some courses myself, or co-directing with my BC counterpart.

I recall that on my first day at post, I felt a brief flash of apprehension at the range of responsibilities awaiting me, until I remembered there'd be a special executive secretary to assist me.

Everyone in the Embassy called her Pani Ania. (Ms. Ania: full name, Anna Wilbik.) This superlative executive secretary was a ray of sunshine in my life, although except for work-elated short trips with her, I never saw her outside the Embassy.

Pani Ania proved capable of dealing with any situation that came along: all Polish correspondence; travel arrangements; appointments with ministry and university officials; and unending requests ranging from "difficult" to "impossible." Throughout them all, she never wavered in her charming but firm manner. She also explained Polish enigmas to me so they seemed logical. She was a multi-talented marvel.

On my very first day, it was Pani Ania who gently and apologetically informed me that Polish teachers of English rarely, if ever, came into the Embassy — and then it was only with special permission from their directors to request supplementary English-teaching materials. Still, I went ahead and brought up stacks of teaching materials from the basement storeroom to display and have on hand to distribute, in case visitors did show up. I looked for better times ahead.

When I'd finally settled into my new place in the Embassy, I often felt lonely and aimlessly free on the weekends. Although I've been a walker all my life, I've never enjoyed walking by myself in strange countries, where this is sometimes misinterpreted as "female on the prowl." In addition, I missed the activities with my teaching colleagues in Turkey, not to mention neighbors, former students, and my large extended family of loving children and relatives-by-marriage.

I did receive invitations to some events in Warsaw, which I always accepted with great pleasure, but these invitations were rare.

And I did, of course, make an effort to study the language. At a neighborhood bookstore, I found several beginning Polish grammar books for English speakers that were well written and helpful. I was able to refresh the basic Polish I'd learned a decade earlier.

I even requested language tutoring from the Embassy roster of available Polish tutors, and was assigned, ironically, a bright young man who'd been in one of my summer English courses ten years earlier. He agreed to have a daily Polish language session with me sitting in a quiet corner of the Embassy cafeteria, an arrangement that continued for some weeks until I finally had to terminate the tutoring. Admittedly, I was not a stellar student in Polish, so I really didn't blame him for yawning now and then, or peeking at his watch so often.

What I privately objected to was his habit of keeping an eye on the Americans coming in and out of the cafeteria when I needed his help with inflected verb forms. It was altogether too disconcerting; he reminded me too much of the "reporter" in a long-ago summer seminar for Polish teachers, who was not really focused on the lesson, but kept slipping in and out of the classroom to report on the group.

So I went back to carrying a bilingual Polish-English pocket dictionary in my handbag wherever I went.

One sunny Saturday morning in Warsaw, I experienced an epiphany — a little voice saying to me: *Your weekends of solitude are really Golden Hours. Spend them wisely!* So when I decided to commit my free weekends to creative writing, *Marty the Martian,* the little play I'd written for students in Turkey, immediately came to mind. I dug up my old notes, and sat down at the kitchen table with my portable typewriter.

Soon, the familiar surge of creative energy took over, and I began working on **Play # 2: *The Television Contest****.* On my free weekends now, I would sometimes type happily for hours, so absorbed in a world of my own that an unexpected telephone ring or knock on the door would almost literally jerk me back to Earth!

Oftentimes, plots for little plays would come to me in my half-sleep. Most of the ideas were simple to outline, but some required a little light research. Then I'd browse until I found what I needed in the Embassy Library. *Submarine*, though, a scenario about fictional submarine research in California, required a bit of technical accuracy and I was forced to look around for help. Luckily, I found an Embassy officer who'd been in the Navy and had served duty on a submarine!

I explained the simple plot and asked him what the motley crew might plausibly be searching for on the ocean floor. Also, could they take their mascot cat down with them?

His first answer was: "How about searching for a sunken ship with a cargo of gold?" And his second answer: "No, they shouldn't take a cat down in a submarine; its ears are too sensitive. But a monkey would work." This was invaluable information!

On another weekend, I was basing a scenario on the classic Grimm Brothers' tale of three farm animals that left the barnyard to seek their fortune in the world. On their way, they frightened a band of robbers counting out gold coins in a deserted house.

That story was easy enough to start, but I couldn't exactly recall which animals were involved, so I took an informal poll of several employees lunching in the Embassy cafeteria. One friend remembered the story well: "Rooster, Donkey, Cat!"

I was doubly pleased: I got the correct answer, and I was learning to use my resources at hand.

For pedagogical reasons, I grouped the little plays:
1. Simple in concept and structures: ***Marty the Martian, Submarine, On the Bus***
2. Advanced in concept and language complexity: ***Sleepy Head, Mr. Fix-It's Repair Shop, The Three Singers, The Opposite Family, The Cat in the Window***.

For the Turkish publisher, I made up several scenarios:
3. Based on Nasreddin Hoca *(pronounced ho-dja)*, the wise old man of Turkish folktales: ***The Hodja and the Tired Mother, The Three Singers, The Hodja's Cat, The Hodja and the Emperor's Elephant.***

Finally, to add variety, I also drafted other scenarios:
4. Based on elements of mystery, melodrama, humor, and vaudeville: ***The Patient Complaints Clerk, A Day in the Life of a Small Park, Airplane, Storm, Mystery at the Blue Lake Hotel, My Darlin' Clementine***, and ***The Perry Family Traveling Show***, a suspenseful, melodramatic play within a play.

The next two years of my ETO assignment in Poland became increasingly active. Empty weekends that at first had been free for my play-writing project became fewer and fewer, as my schedule filled with weekend seminars in different regions of the country.

This involved a lot of travel. Some programs were specifically for American Fulbright grantees teaching English in Eastern Europe; others were multi-national programs for English teachers from Eastern Europe, sponsored jointly by the British Council and the U.S. State Department. Travel preparations and follow-ups were always complicated and time-consuming.

After these exhilarating but tiring tours, it was only now and then that I could rest and spend a rare weekend in my quiet apartment. Then I would concentrate even more eagerly on the growing number of *Plays for the English-Language Classroom (working title).* By my third year in Warsaw, I'd written 19 plays during my free weekends, and was now putting finishing touches on a manuscript to send to Istanbul. The manuscript's final title would be: **"*Easy Plays in English.*"**

One evening, I took a break from typing plays when my British Council counterpart invited me to a lecture for local Polish teachers of English. I always found the methodology lectures stimulating, as well as practical for the teachers to use in their own classrooms.

Also, it was exciting to sit in an audience of such experienced British and Polish academics. I'd met a number of the Polish teachers at our seminars in past years, but nowadays I never had an opportunity to see them except for these British lecture occasions.

The British, I should point out, had no restrictions on travel or contact with Poles. Yet, at the same time, Polish authorities were exercising more restrictions against Americans each year, specifically those working in the American Embassy. So, especially for me, it was a treat to be invited to a British Council lecture where I could mingle with teaching colleagues occasionally.

On one such pleasant lecture evening, I was enjoying a cup of tea during intermission when I recognized the head of the English Department of Warsaw University in a group of people across the room. This Polish professor who spoke elegant British English was married to an Englishwoman; both were established textbook writers. Some of their books, in fact, were sitting on my bookshelf.

The professor came over to greet me, politely inquiring after my health. Then, quietly, he asked me what I was doing in my free time. I thought either he was simply curious, or this was his gentle way of indicating he knew I had no social life to speak of.

"Oh," I said, fumbling for words, "I write. . ." My voice trailed off vaguely into silence. I just couldn't finish the sentence.

This seemed to pique his interest. "What do you write?" he asked in his polite — and kindly — voice.

"Well, I'm working on little plays for the English-language class-room, with lots of characters so all the students can take part." Suddenly, I felt rather intimidated by his academic textbook-publishing reputation, and I just didn't feel up to finishing that sentence, either.

"I'd love to see it!" he said quietly. I took this to be polite small talk from a very polite gentleman. I smiled, nodded, and put it out of my mind.

It took me longer than I'd expected to type up a final manuscript for Önder bey, the teacher/bookstore owner in Istanbul. I'd promised to send him a copy for review sometime in the fall. Now I realized how swiftly the weeks were passing. Autumn leaves were already falling and some trees were almost bare.

I'd become very busy with my regular duties, so my writing project had to wait until my next free weekend. Then, I not only had to finish typing the manuscript, I needed to prepare a carefully detailed cover-letter with a prospectus explaining the purpose, academic level, instructions for the teachers, and so on.

More weeks passed. In the meantime, Pani Ania received word that I was invited to another evening of British Council lectures for teachers of English.

It was more or less the same academic crowd, eager to listen to lectures on the latest trends in language teaching. As always, the Polish teachers welcomed the opportunity to converse and socialize in English, while enjoying tea and refreshments. The quiet professor was there, as usual, and I nodded to him politely. He moved unobtrusively through the crowd to stand at the refreshment table, where I was helping myself to a cup of tea. In his quiet and polite manner, the professor inquired about my health, as usual. Then he asked about the progress of my plays. The last evening lecture seemed so long ago I was surprised he'd remembered my mentioning the plays at all. I admit I felt flattered.

"I've just finished 19 plays, and I hope to send a draft off to Istanbul next week," I told him.

"I wonder, Mrs. Malkoç, if you would be kind enough to let *me* look at your draft before you send it?" he murmured quietly. "Your secretary knows my secretary, and they can arrange it."

What could I say? He sounded quite serious, so I could only answer graciously, "Of course. Tomorrow morning." He thanked me with a quiet smile; we shook hands and departed.

My secretary and the Professor's secretary were indeed close friends. That they shared a lot of confidences, I was sure. When I brought my manuscript in a large manila envelope the next morning and handed it to Pani Ania, she was obviously expecting it. Without a word, she took the envelope and left the room.

At first, I took it as a great compliment that such a distinguished textbook writer would want to look at my writing, but again, I dismissed it as a gesture of professional courtesy. Or curiosity.

I couldn't take time wondering about that now, however; it was time to plan my home leave. I hoped to spend Christmas holiday with my family in Washington State.

All those past free weekends, I'd been doing so much typing and retyping of the final draft of the plays that I'd memorized the familiar lines: I could hear the voices of the characters in my head. This led to another epiphany:

To learn another language well, to be able to speak *the new language, you really have to* hear it spoken.

Question: How can these little plays help the students speak *English?*

Answer: With a listening tape that sounds like Radio Theater!

At the time I was writing ***Easy Plays in English*** *(final title),* I was quite familiar with EFL (English as a Foreign Language) listening tapes that were available for students at that time. The commercial tapes in the bookshops were recorded by the authors themselves or by EFL teachers who simply read the lines from their books.

While these tapes provided clear pronunciation guides to words and phrases, they were often read mechanically. I wanted to provide everyday American English speech closer to actual conversation — to create *realistic* listening tapes. I was convinced they would greatly enhance the impact and dimensions of ***Easy Plays***.

When I first got the idea to record the plays, I thought immediately of my youngest daughter, Melike [meh-lee-keh, who had studied drama earlier at the Cornish School of Arts in Seattle, and was now taking drama classes at the University of Washington. She knew a lot of budding actors.

So I immediately wrote her a note outlining my plans.

Dear Melike,

I'm arriving in Seattle the week before Christmas with a new "shoestring recording project." I want to record my little plays for English teaching, copy enclosed. Do you think you can help me with the following?

1. Round up a dozen actors to record the lines, for a stipend of $50 each. I will have bank drafts made out when I get to Seattle.
2. Make copies of the plays for the actors.
3. Find an inexpensive recording studio, with stereo-quality mikes.
4. Look up Jan Cyr (family friend, not far from Seattle) who is professionally experienced in sound effects, voice-overs, and laying down background music. I'd like her to help me make top-quality stereo recordings, like Radio Theater, to accompany my plays. We can discuss her fee when we meet. She might like a trip to Istanbul.

Will you be the co-director with me? Love, Mother

Carefully, I put a carbon copy of the plays into a strong manila envelope with my note, and air-expressed it to Seattle. . . .

Now my schedule of teaching workshops, including one in Bucharest, was busier than ever, filling my weekdays and my weekends. The last leaves of autumn had fallen and the cold, snowy days of winter were approaching. This was a reminder to me of my promise to Önder bey, the teacher/bookstore owner in Istanbul. It also reminded me of my manuscript. Where on earth was it?

There had been no word at all from the Polish professor. I asked Pani Ania to please call Pani Mila to find our about the manuscript. The next day, word came back: "The Committee are still reading it." Now, here was a real-world mystery! Who was *The Committee?* And why were *they* looking at my precious manuscript? Were they Polish censors? The manuscript has nothing to do with Poland! Önder bey is waiting for it in Turkey! But this was no time to delve into mysteries, I thought; the Thanksgiving holiday had arrived.

As usual, Thanksgiving was celebrated quietly by the Americans in the Embassy in small private cliques, and in large group dinners that included "loners" like me. Although it was a nostalgic time for most people, we all enjoyed the turkey and trimmings as well as the holiday spirit. Following Thanksgiving, a lull set in then, and people were gearing up for the harsh weather predicted ahead. I completed my workshops as scheduled; schools and universities finished up their courses before the end-of-year break and the Christmas-New Year holiday.

My personal plans were also shaping up: I'd be flying from Warsaw to Seattle, Washington, with a week's stop-over in Seattle first to visit my two younger daughters, Melike and Kâmuran. I'd timed this visit to coincide with the University's Christmas break and my tape-recording project. From Seattle, I'd fly on to my hometown of Spokane, to spend Christmas with my oldest daughter Hikmet, my son Timur, and myriad relatives. Miraculously, by the time I arrived in Seattle, Melike had managed to recruit a cast of multi-talented students, plus one of her instructors. He had agreed to record out of curiosity, I suspect; it was a wonderful stroke of good fortune to have him in the group. As it turned out, his deep baritone voice was the most marvelously versatile of all the volunteer recorders; he read a wide variety of roles, each in a totally different and captivating voice.

As soon as the UW drama students understood that middle-school students in faraway Turkey would be listening to the cassettes to perfect their American-English pronunciation, they threw themselves wholeheartedly into the project, and achieved so much more than I'd hoped for, I was *thrilled*. I felt like a composer must feel when, under an orchestra conductor's direction, the musicians bring the composer's music notes to life. I was *elated!*

It took multiple mikes and several full days working under pressure in Michael Lord's basement studio in Seattle, for the dozen or so recording students to finish reading the 19 plays. On their last day, they all signed the release forms I'd prepared, giving me permission to use their voices. They received their stipends gracefully, and went off to celebrate a happy Christmas.

The next recording component was the background music: an expert (and family friend) Jan Cyr helped me with selecting the music, and then advised me on details for legal permissions and payments. She also did all the simple sound effects herself. It was my great good fortune that this versatile professional in sound recording was willing to take on such an unusual recording project, especially given the limited and hurried-up time frame.

Even the studio owner, Mike Lord, got into the spirit of the project. He worked late into the night to finish editing the 19 recordings with their sound effects and music. Then he personally drove the three master reel-to-reel tapes, with copies, packed for registered special delivery to the Seattle airport post office, to be expressed to my friends in Tulsa, Oklahoma. *(This was my usual stopover when returning to post from home-leave in Spokane; my husband and I had been married in Tulsa, and our first daughter, Hikmet, was born there.)*

This time, it was not simply a sentimental visit to see old college friends Bill and Kathryn Brownfield; they were arranging with a Tulsa recording company to make multiple cassette copies for me. During my stopover; I would pick up the copies. The recording company agreed to keep the master reels in special storage for me in their warehouse until further notice.

I was deliriously happy with the results of the recording sessions, and could hardly believe that everything went as smoothly as planned on my home leave: the visits with my daughters in Seattle, with my sister and siblings in Spokane, and with my old college friends in Tulsa. The return flight back to Warsaw and my work-a-day world was smooth and "uneventful."

"Welcome back!" Pani Ania smiled, the minute I walked into my office. She waited a split second to announce: "The State Pedagogical Textbook Publishing House of Warsaw sent you a letter this morning."

This was some kind of thunderbolt, I could tell from her voice. Something serious. "I requested an Embassy car for you," she went on. "It's waiting outside, and I would be happy to accompany you," adding that there was nothing else on my calendar for the day.

My trust in Pani Ania was absolute: I knew she would eventually make these cryptic announcements clear to me at some point — once we were out of range of the ubiquitous listening devices planted by Polish security.

I simply nodded in agreement, turned around without a word, and walked back out the door. Ania accompanied me silently, and together we walked to the Embassy parking space where our favorite driver, Pan Tadeusz, was waiting. With a smile, he opened my car door, then Pani Ania's, and drove us the short distance in silence to our destination, parking discretely on a side street. Again, he assisted with our doors, and nodded slightly to indicate he would be waiting. In continuing silence, Ania and I trudged up the long flight of stairs to the main offices of the State Pedagogical Textbook Publishing House.

Up until now, entering *any* official Polish government building always gave me a slight chill of trepidation, partly because I understood so little Polish and this made me feel vulnerable. This morning, however, I noticed that Ania was smiling back at the row of smiling faces in the glassed-in offices we were passing, and she was exchanging greetings with them as well! It seemed as if everyone there knew Pani Ania, and what we were about. I was the only one in the dark.

At the outer office, we stopped so Pani Ania could introduce several people. I responded politely, I hoped. A smiling woman at an outer desk said quietly, "They're waiting for you." I followed Ania to a door at the end of the corridor. She knocked and went in. I followed.

Here, my memory is too dim for faces, but I do remember sitting down at a table, and someone placing a legal-sized document in front of me. Ania was explaining something, and asking something.

The scene seemed so surreal I had to take a deep breath to clear my head. The well-dressed man behind the inner desk began speaking and Ania translated:

"The Committee would like to publish your book, Mrs. Malkoç. What do you say?"

"Oh!" I said, "I'm *surprised!"* Fortunately, I thought to myself, I'm sitting down, or I'd fall over!

I took another deep breath, and gave a pleased little laugh, as if this were an everyday occurrence.

Ania continued. "They want to know: do you hold the copyright?"

"Copyright?" I was coming back to Earth. "Yes, I do," then quickly added: "That is, I haven't given the copyright to anyone, yet. I promised a Turkish publisher that he could print the book as soon as I send it to him. But he will have a copyright for Turkey only." I was beginning to think more clearly now.

"And is there any copyright material in the book?"

"No, there is no copyright material in the book," I replied. "The long poem, *Annabel Lee,* is by Edgar Allan Poe, who died in 1849. No copyright permission is necessary; it's in the Public Domain. Also, the old songs: *My Darlin' Clementine, For He's a Jolly Good Fellow,* and *Looby Loo,* are all in the Public Domain. I made a list of them for the cassette labels." I was pausing after each statement while Pani Ania translated, then I added: "I've just had the plays recorded on stereo cassette tapes, with background music, and I've taken care of the copyright permissions for the cassette music."

The rest of that visit involved a lengthy explanation of the terms of payment in Polish *zloty* at the going rate, the initial print run (2,000 copies, as I recall) and the number of author's copies (which I don't recall). I do remember finally signing multiple copies of the contract, and asking to have a galley proof so I could personally proof-read it.

That evening, I brewed a pot of tea and sat down at my kitchen table where I had typed up so many pages of *Easy Plays* on my free weekends. As I poured myself a cup, the kaleidoscope of the day's events flashed through my mind and I tried to put everything into some kind of order.

Relaxing over another cup, I suddenly remembered my Agency's official policy about employees writing for outside publication: it should be cleared and approved of by one's Agency director.

When the first galley proofs arrived several weeks later, I immediately carried them over to the director's office at the end of the hall, to show him and advise him of the offer from the State Publishing House. He was quite pleased, I could tell, and said there was no personal, political, or religious content in the writing, so there should be no problem at all with having my English-teaching material published in Poland. On the contrary, he reminded me: English teaching material is part of my assignment. I gave a little sigh of relief.

My next task would be proofreading the first galleys from the Polish State Textbook Publishing House. The thought of this familiar task calmed me to sleep that night.

It was on a Sunday morning when I first spread the large galley pages out on the extended kitchen table and then checked each page, line by line, slowly and painstakingly. I wrote down my editing notes in as clear a fashion as possible. I knew that the Polish publishing house editors were highly trained, excellent editors, but this was an unusual textbook, in English, that required unusual play formatting. I wrote out a kind of style sheet for my formatting, and American English spelling. Finally, Pani Ania arranged to have the pages returned to the publishing house.

After the passage of time, one's memory dims, but it is safe to say that some months passed while the book went through various stages of formatting, illustrating, and printing in final form. One day, Pani Ania requested one sample cassette for the publishing house to listen to for a quality check. On another day, the recording office contacted her to ask if, as I had promised, a master set of the tape cassettes was available. She reassured them, and made an appointment for Pan Tadeusz to drive me to deliver the recordings I'd brought from Tulsa, Oklahoma. These would now be the master cassettes for the local technician to copy from, in order to reproduce sets of cassettes. (The dialogues recorded for one book filled up three cassettes).

This Warsaw technician was a "private expert," I was told, and did this special work in his home. I can still see him in my mind's eye, rushing out to welcome me in his garden, smiling and shaking my hand vigorously, while complimenting me on the stereo quality of the sample tape I had sent him. He could sit and listen to the *Easy Plays in English* sample cassette all day long!

It is safe to say that another interval of several months passed; I was involved in preparing for programs in Eastern Europe, and making travel arrangements during one of the coldest winters in many years. As always, with Pani Ania's careful eye to details during the preparation stages (leaving nothing to chance), all the arrangements were carried out smoothly, and the seminars were always stimulating and enriching for the participants.

At the end of the seminar circuit, and the end of a busy day writing up reports back in the office, Pani Ania brought in a large package for me wrapped in grey recycled paper and stamped: *Polish State Textbook Publishing House.* In my inner excitement, I don't even remember how I got the package home that day, probably Pan Tadeusz drove me home, because I never would have gotten it home on a streetcar.

Fortunately, I was free that weekend, so I devoted myself entirely to proofreading for any occasional errors (I found none), admiring the delightful illustrations, and pinching myself in disbelief that *Easy Plays in English* was actually in print! That I was actually looking at author's copies of the text and a set of cassettes labeled: *"Published by State Pedagogical Textbook Publishing, Warsaw, 1988."* All weekend, I was floating on Cloud Nine.

*EPILOGUE One of the first letters I received was from an English teacher in Krakow, who wrote to me with her compliments, and mentioned how popular the **Easy Plays** cassettes were in her classes. "All that my students want to do in English class is listen to your cassettes!" Thinking back to that modest recording specialist in*

110

Warsaw, I'm convinced that he and his studio-quality equipment were responsible for the excellent sound quality of the reproductions in Poland.

Sad to say, this was in contrast to the reproductions in Turkey, where the copying must have been done hastily, on someone's poor-quality home-recorder or "boom box." For the most part, those tapes were quite unintelligible. I shed tears of frustration and anger, not only because the teachers who bought them with their hard-earned money would be disappointed, but because I was ashamed to have my name appearing on the labels.

Fortunately, the Istanbul teacher/bookstore-owner/publisher had engaged a well-known artist who did really fine illustrations; also fortunately, he had publicized the book in many venues. But then, unfortunately, he distributed free copies to a large number of teachers. In so doing, he must have lost a lot of money. I know that as the author, I never received a cent — or kurush —for the book, and I never heard from that publisher again.

To the Polish artist/caricaturist, Julian Bohdanowicz of Warsaw, I wrote a grateful letter of thanks for his lighthearted and delightful illustrations in **Easy Plays in English.** With just a few strokes of pen and ink, he set the scenes, and captured the spirit of youthful make-believe and whimsy. I felt deeply honored to have my little plays illustrated by such a famous and insightful artist.

In Poland, there were various repercussions from the plays. I received a number of invitations from English teachers to attend their students' performances. I was extremely pleased to think that my plays were actually being performed by schoolchildren in Poland. I was thrilled, in fact. That was my greatest reward.

To these kind invitations, all I could tactfully reply was that I would be very pleased to accept an _official_ invitation, and then I would be very happy to attend. I did not wish to jeopardize the teachers, who may not have heard that I was not exactly in favor with the Communist Party officials.

Following my response to one teacher's earlier invitation, he made a train trip all the way from Krakow in central Poland to dis-invite me, and to apologize because his school director would not give him permission to invite me to his students' performance. There were tears in his eyes as he told me this, and he nearly broke down. I'll admit I had a large lump in my throat, and I struggled to stifle the anger in my heart against the regime.

So, word was spreading, apparently, that the **Easy Plays** author was not only an American, but was employed in the American Embassy! I should point out here that the combination of my first two given names was also a popular combination for girls in Poland, and my Turkish married name was often taken as Slavic. In addition, there was no attribution anywhere in **Easy Plays** to indicate my origin or place of employment. In hindsight, I think this may have been cleverly deliberate oversight on the part of the Warsaw publishing house. If so, to them I say "Bravo."

Another Polish teacher wrote an emotional letter, saying she regretted being unable to invite me to see her class perform scenes from **Easy Plays**. She had no camera to take a picture, she said, but she was enclosing colored crayon pictures her students had drawn to illustrate the scenes they'd performed in. I still treasure those precious little pictures; just remembering them and their dedicated teacher brings a lump to my throat.

There were several occasions to which I was formally invited by letter, then officially dis-invited by telephone, but not as a direct consequence of **Easy Plays**. One occasion in particular I remember well because it was a meeting of many English instructors, directors, and Ministry of Education people in Poznan. I was looking forward to attending the meeting the next day.

Late that afternoon (of the day before the meeting), Pani Ania received an urgent call from the Poznan University secretary announcing that the meeting had been suddenly called off. Pani Ania immediately cancelled my early morning train ticket.

An evening or two later, I had occasion to phone my British Council counterpart about an unrelated matter. His wife answered the phone and said she was expecting her husband back from the big meeting in Poznan any time now; he would call me the minute he was home. I'll admit I did see the ironic humor in the wife's innocently dropping the information about the "cancelled" meeting, but I was more exasperated than anything else with the transparently deceitful games people had to play to keep in the good graces of the Communist Party officials. . . .

Some years have passed. Poland has changed much since the Berlin Wall was torn down and there is no longer an Iron Curtain cutting off that part of the world. I'm happy that is so, for the sake of all the good people I remember in Poland, especially when I think of that beautiful

112

country with its long history of partition heartaches. And always, the first person who comes to mind is lovely Ania Wilbik, who made my life bearable and bright.

A final word about the ultimate fate of **Easy Plays in English***. When I retired and returned to live in my hometown of Spokane, Washington, I revised the book with the help of David Clemmons, a talented art instructor at Spokane Falls Community College. He delicately Americanized the characters and glamorized the cover. I deleted several of the Turkish plays, keeping only one of the Turkish folktale scenarios. Ultimately, Regents / Prentice-Hall / Pearson published it for international distribution in 1993.*

Not surprisingly, with the normal passage of time, the advent and rapid evolution of computers, videos, cell phones and text messaging, **Easy Plays** *has become out-of-date. Such is life.*

In my heart, however, **Easy Plays** *remains enshrined as a bittersweet memory of my unforgettable seven years in Poland.*

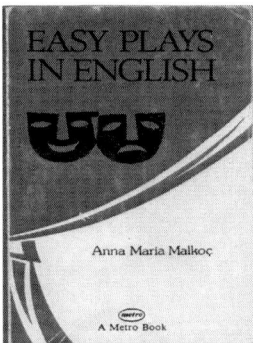

Metro Books Publishing Istanbul, 1985

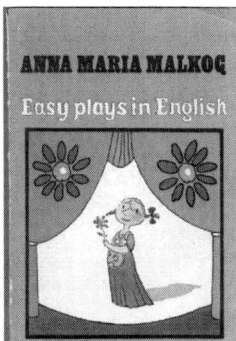

Warsaw State Textbook Publishing, 1986

113

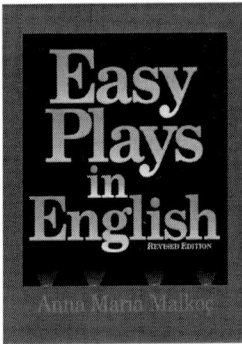

Regents/Prentice-Hall/Pearson, Englewood Cliffs, NJ 1993

114

12

YOU *MUST* REFUSE THRICE
Istanbul, Turkey 1985

*PROLOGUE   On my last trip to Istanbul, I had missed seeing Münire,
and I vowed to make a special effort to see her the next time I was on
her side of the Bosphorus — the strait separating the European side of
Turkey, from the Asian or Anatolian side. At the time, I was working in
English-teaching seminars in Poland, so it was a relatively short plane
hop to Istanbul during my free time.*

*Although I was fond of all my former students from the
teacher-training institute in Ankara where I first knew Münire, she had
earned a special place in my heart. After my husband's death, Münire
had stayed with me and helped me with my pre-teen children. In the
years since, she became a full-fledged English teacher, favored by her
director, respected by her colleagues, beloved by her students. I called
her to tell her I'd be in Istanbul that week. She invited me to dinner.*

Münire answered the door with an enthusiastic shout: "Oh,
Mrs. Malkoç! Welcome! Please come in! I have a surprise
for you!" It seemed ages since my last visit to Istanbul. . . .

*Welcoming Munire and a Gazi classmate
to the first tea party at my apartment in Ankara.*

Munire indicated a chair for me to sit in, and excused herself to stir
something in the kitchen. Naturally, I looked about for the "surprise."

What I saw was the dinner table loaded with platters of my
favorite dishes: grape leaves stuffed with rice, green bell peppers
stuffed with minced meat, savory meatballs, eggplant baked in tomato
sauce, white cheese pastries with parsley, rice pilav sprinkled with pine
nuts and black currants. And, of course, a large plate of baklava — a
traditional kind of strudel with honeyed walnuts.

116

"No, it's not the dinner table. *Here's* the surprise!" she said, opening another door so her smiling mother could step out. Now, that *was* a surprise. I knew it takes hours to go from one outlying district of Istanbul to another, especially if it involves crossing the Bosporus strait by ferryboat, and that's a real expedition for someone her mother's age.

I hadn't seen Münire's mother, Naciye hanim, for a *very* long time, and I was touched that she had come all this way today. I knew she visited her daughter on a regular basis, and most probably she came to help out with the cooking.

"*Hos geldiniz!*" she welcomed me, and I responded with "*Hos bulduk!*" the polite response, as a welcomed guest should. We hugged and kissed, both of us bubbling over with news to exchange and questions to ask. I quickly freshened up for dinner, and Münire showed us our seats at the table.

Looking at their dear, smiling faces and the platters piled high with their delicious food, I was overcome with nostalgia — and hunger pangs. Even with her mother's help, I knew that it must have taken hours and hours, if not days, to do all the stuffing and rolling and baking involved in this cooking. Could I do justice to this feast, I wondered. Well, I was certainly going to try 1

Mother and daughter began to ply me with food, making sure I had at least a small taste from each platter. As I sampled the delectable dishes, I recalled my first encounter with a typical Turkish dinner, family style, and I smiled at the memory.

"Mrs. Malkoç, do you like the *dolma* (stuffed grape leaves)?"

"Oh, yes, these are delicious, Münire! Health to your hands!" (*This compliment to the cook was one I had to repeat often during the dinner.*)

"Actually, Munire," I told her, "I was just recalling the big family welcome when my husband, Baby Hikmet, and I first arrived in Istanbul in 1953. There were so many relatives, and everyone speaking Turkish, all so happy to see Selahattin after seven years of studying abroad. . . . *May he rest in peace!*

I'll never forget that family dinner. When we all sat down at the table, the first course was absolutely the best lentil soup I'd ever tasted in my life. It was so delicious that when they asked if I would like more, I said '*Evet!*' [Yes!] My vocabulary was limited to about ten words at the time.

I had no idea there would be so many courses to come, and I was really full after the second bowl of soup. Today, of course, I know I should have said '*Tesekkur ederim, hayir.*'" ('Thank you; no, thank you.') I laughed at the memory of myself. "I've learned a lot about Turkish table manners since I came to Turkey so long ago!" *(By now, I'd learned enough Turkish to carry on a simple conversation.)*

Münire and her mother joined me in laughing, though apparently with quite different memories in mind. In fact, her mother confessed shyly: "Yes, and I learned a lot about American table manners too!"

"What did you learn, *Teyze*?" (Auntie) I asked, in great curiosity. She was smiling again, at the recollection.

"Do you remember the first time I came to visit Münire when she was at your house in Ankara?"

"Oh, yes," I said. "I remember very well! You arrived on the evening train, and I prepared a dinner plate for you. I said, 'Your dinner is ready.' But you said, 'No, thank you.'

Then, I thought you must be terribly tired, too tired to eat. So I put the food away in the refrigerator so it wouldn't spoil, and you could eat it later if you wished. Then you just went to bed."

"Yes, that's right. You put the food away, and I just went to bed." She was laughing softly as she recalled this scene.

"And," I continued, because I had a vivid memory of her visit, "early the next morning I walked over to get bread fresh from the bakery, and I prepared breakfast with buttered toast, honey, soft boiled eggs, and fresh tea for you. But, you said, 'No, thank you' to the breakfast! I thought perhaps you didn't like the way I cooked eggs. Then I had to go to my English classes, and I never got to ask how you were feeling that day. So, tell me now, *Teyze (Auntie)*: What was it that you learned about American manners at my house?"

She had to stop laughing to answer my question: "I learned that Americans only ask you once!"

"Once? When?" I was really puzzled.

"When they offer you food!" She could tell I was too puzzled to get the point, and she had to explain further. "It's not polite for me to accept food if you only offer it once. You should offer *more* than once. To be *really* polite, you should offer three times. Then I can accept politely." Finally, I got the point: I should have *insisted* — although I think Americans, as a general rule, don't like such insistence over food. But, we all had a good laugh together, then returned to happier reminiscing, nibbling our way through the delicacies.

May Allah's beneficence always be in abundance!

EPILOGUE   *Later, I pondered the advice on Turkish table manners from Münire's mother. Is this, I wondered, some regional custom that I never ran into in all my years in Turkey? I was still pondering this when Münire took me to the train station. I had a ticket for the night train to Ankara, where I would be staying with my brother-in-law Muammer and his wife Nezihe the next day. I decided I would ask them about Turkish table manners. Both Muammer and Nezihe are direct and forthcoming, and I value their opinions.*

When the train pulled into the Ankara station next morning, there was dear Muammer waiting to pick me up. I always felt a great rush of nostalgia walking up the steps to their vine-covered front porch, and entering their living room with the comfortable sofa. I thought of all the times over the years I had sat there with Nezihe on those velvet cushions, sipping her aromatic Turkish coffee sweetened perfectly to taste!

But now it was breakfast time, and as I put down my travel things and moved past the open kitchen, I could see Nezihe's teapot steeping atop the teakettle, and the row of tea glasses lined up on the counter, ready to be filled. In the adjacent family room, three place settings were already laid out on the table, with the family's favorite breakfast assortments. They were waiting breakfast for me.

The familiar crystal dishes, I saw, were full of white and yellow cheese, fresh butter, honey, cherry jam, black and green olives. The little porcelain plates held slices of ripe red tomatoes and fresh green cucumbers. The wicker basket held slices of traditional Turkish bread fresh from the morning bakery, covered with a linen napkin. The crystal bowl of sugar cubes, the little teaspoon holder, and a stack of folded paper napkins sat next to the breadbasket. It was the familiar "help yourself" family arrangement. I've always found the typical Turkish breakfast a delightfully satisfying morning meal, as well as healthfully nutritious. I enjoy it all, thoroughly.

On this particular morning, I thought it polite to wait until at least the second glass of tea before asking any questions about Turkish table etiquette. It was polite to ask about the family first. So, I asked about Muammer and Nezihe themselves. Then, how was their daughter Sirin, [sheer-in] who lived on the outskirts of Ankara? Her husband Ali? Their young son Caner? [John-air]

And their son Serdar [sair-dahr] Malkoç in Izmir? And his wife Birsen? [beer-sen] Their young son Alper? [all-pair] in college?

We were actually having our third glass of breakfast tea before I felt it was acceptable to bring up the topic of table etiquette. Rather than phrasing a question, I described Naciye hanim's (Münire's

*mother's) visit, and then asked if she was typical of people in Bolu —
the small town in the mountains south of Istanbul where their family
comes from.*

*I was really curious about Munire's mother, so I began to describe her
visit, and how she politely refused to eat any food in my house: none at
dinner and none at breakfast. She told me you had to offer her food
three times before she would accept it. Is this a regional custom? Or, I
asked, is it some kind of a religious restriction, perhaps?*

*Muammer, who had been listening intently, and nodding from
time to time, couldn't contain himself any longer. He finally burst out
laughing. "I always tell everyone to watch out when they visit Anna
Maria's house!" He became totally overcome by another fit of
laughing, and struggled to calm himself so he could say something else.*

*"I tell them to answer 'YES' if Anna Maria asks if they would
like food or drink. If she offers you anything to eat or drink, say 'YES,
please,' right away! Otherwise, she'll put it all away in the
refrigerator!" And he was again lost in another paroxysm of laughter.*

*"Muammer, is that true?" Nezihe was caught up in
Muammer's infectious laugh, and started giggling.*

*"Oh, yes!" Muammer stopped laughing long enough to answer
her. "The first time when I came up by train from the oilfields and
stayed overnight at her house in Ankara, I went to bed hungry! I was
too polite!" He wiped his eyes and slowly regained his composure as
Nezihe refilled our tea glasses.*

*I had to giggle a little, myself. But secretly, I wish I'd been
alerted to this point of Turkish etiquette long ago.*

13

The BALTIC RESTAURANT
Gdansk, Poland 1985

PROLOGUE *People say that travel is broadening: by observing what is going on around you, you may learn about other cultures and ways of living. I find that to be so true.*

Less obviously, I also find that by studying your own reactions to unfamiliar situations, you may learn about yourself, as I did in a Polish restaurant one lonely Saturday afternoon.

I finished my long weekend workshop for the high school teachers of English in Gdansk on Saturday afternoon, and waved them goodbye as they departed for various districts in the north of Poland. Then I headed back to my hotel. It had been hours since breakfast, and I was hungry. Rather than returning to the coffee shop in my overnight hotel, I decided to look for a restaurant within walking distance, with a view of the Baltic Sea.

The only eating place within sight was set back from the road running along the coastline and through the city of Gdansk (still called *Danzig* by the German tourists). The restaurant itself was one enormous room, with imposingly high ceilings, from an era before the advent of the later stolid, blockish Stalinist architecture. This was evident from the graceful touches imparted by the many French windows, occasional potted plants, and crisp white table linens. The place seemed well suited for the summer tourists who came to sun themselves by the sea; by now, however, they all seemed to have disappeared with the onset of the crisp autumn weather. When I entered, there was no *maitre d'* or server to be seen, so I headed for the far corner of the room, where a wide window faced the Baltic.

After all the teachers left, I was in a rather melancholy mood, and thought I might as well enjoy the seascape, at least. There's such grandeur in the vast sweep of the Baltic from this perspective: it's enough to inspire a painter or a poet. I decided to *savor* my solitude.

An attentive server soon appeared at my table, welcomed me to the establishment, and with a smile, gently motioned me to a table toward the middle of the wide room. Quietly, he was saying something to me that was beyond my basic Polish, but somehow, I got the message that the secluded corner I'd headed for was not an appropriate location for me. Perhaps it was his subtle frown as he shook his head ever so slightly, with the barest hint of disapproval on his face. Not quite sure of his message, I simply nodded, picked up my briefcase and followed him to the center table. *(Much later on, back in Warsaw, someone who knew the restaurant well delicately advised me that the corner table was always reserved for "ladies of the night.")*

A few guests were straggling out of the restaurant as I came in, and all the other tables were empty at this post-midday dinner hour. I took my time looking over the menu, choosing mushroom soup, the fish of the day with boiled potatoes, and a compote from the dessert menu. When the savory soup arrived, I lingered over it to the last spoonful, gazing out the side windows where the panoramic seacoast could be seen in veiled shades of gray. In the far distance, I saw seagulls swooping and soaring in silence and a dark freighter edging its way east along the rim of the horizon.

My thoughts meandered: *How gray the sea is, and how flat. There's no wind to ruffle up the waves, no tides coming in, or going out. I wondered idly: How many different seas have I seen in my life?*

I was still pondering this question when the polite server with the kind voice approached, a group of people in his wake. He stopped, and asked permission to seat them at my table.

I looked up from boning my fish, and glanced around at the huge room full of empty tables. My first reaction was: *What an intrusion of my privacy!* But I'd been in Poland long enough to realize this would have been terribly impolite. Here people shared space graciously. I think not to do so would have been totally unacceptable.

"Madame is alone," the well-meaning server added in Polish. I could see he thought he was rescuing me from my loneliness. In reality, in the mood I was in — missing my teen-age children in boarding school in England, and still grieving for my late husband — the situation was simply adding to my depression.

I knew I needed to work this out in my own way. I needed to get used to being alone now, and to find my equilibrium, but not in the midst of happy strangers whose language presented yet another struggle for me.

Harboring these ungracious thoughts, I could only nod my head in assent, and busy myself with the fish bones while the family was being seated at the end of my long table. I struggled to overcome my unreceptive attitude, which was not at all my usual congenial manner. Instead, I forced myself to look up, smile and greet them with a *"Dzien dobry!"* (Good afternoon.)

A chorus of *"Dzien dobry!"* came from the family in response. Looking up at them directly, I saw a nuclear, fair-haired and blue-eyed family: the youngish-looking father and mother, the little schoolgirl, and the dignified grandfather somewhat older than myself. They were all smiling at me. Instinctively, I smiled back. Then, not wanting to encourage a conversation, I returned to the fish, reflectively and contemplatively, with my eyes on the horizon. By now the dark freighter was out of sight, but a small motorboat was now making its way toward shore.

"Does Madame speak Polish?" asked the grandfather, seated across from me. I shook my head. I could understand his question, and could also answer it in Polish, but knowing so little of the language, I knew I'd soon exhaust my vocabulary. I *longed* to be elsewhere.

"Do you speak English?" came the grandfather's next question.

This time, I responded with a small smile. "Yes, I speak English." What else could I say, politely? I began seriously attacking the potatoes cooling on my plate.

This positive response encouraged the grandfather to make another attempt. He turned to his granddaughter sitting quietly at his side, and asked her in English: "How old are you?"

"I am ten years old," she answered in her high, sweet voice, as if reading from her schoolbook.

"And where do you learn English?"

"I learn English at school." The pair continued their catechism, with the child dutifully responding to the doting grandfather's questions. I could see he was showing off his granddaughter, while attempting to entice me into conversation in English.

The disinterested parents, seated at the far end of the table, were quietly holding their own private conversation. My attention wandered to the side window and the vehicles passing on the road, mostly freight conveyances.

The polite server returned with a large tray loaded with steaming dishes for the family. He unloaded them deftly, then with a flourish announced in Polish, "*Smacznego!*" ("Bon appétit!")

The hungry family did so with great gusto, laughing and passing plates to and fro, sharing tastes from all the dishes. Until their appetites were appeased, there was a welcome lull in the conversation.

From time to time, the server glanced in my direction as he passed, to monitor my progress in dining. As I was on the last of the potatoes and garnish of sliced cucumbers, I looked up, caught his eye, and nodded; at the signal, he unobtrusively removed my empty plates. By now, the grandfather had resumed testing the little girl's English, eliciting the numbers from 1 to 10, the primary colors, and now the days of the week.

124

Dessert — a rhubarb compote and wafer — arrived in a small glass bowl on a porcelain plate. I centered my attention on the rhubarb, eating the stewed plant slowly, relishing its odd tartness. When the server passed again, I silently signaled for my check.

The grandfather, meantime, had apparently run out of categories to test in English. He paused and pulled a gold watch from his watch pocket. "Here," he said to the child in English, "What is this?"

"It is a watch," she replied automatically, looking at him for approval. "It is three o'clock."

"Yes. Very good!" He patted her hand and gave a little sigh. Turning toward me, he held out the watch. "I got this in Chicago."

"It's a beautiful watch," I said, looking at it intently. "Really *beautiful*."

"Yes, I worked many years in Chicago; my company gave it to me. Do you know Chicago?"

"I visited Chicago once. It was exciting. I remember they called it the Windy City."

The grandfather sighed again, at old memories, I imagine. I nodded, politely. At this point in the faltering conversation, the server came by with my check. I settled on the spot, and stood up. As was the custom, I addressed the whole family and said *"Dzienkuje"* (Thank you), a signal that I was leaving the table.

Then my basic teacher's instinct suddenly prompted me to say something to the little girl who had so dutifully responded in English. She was looking directly at me, waiting.

With a serious smile, I leaned toward her and said, slowly and clearly, "You are a *good* girl. And your *English* is *very good!*" I picked up my briefcase, adding another small smile and a dramatic "Goodbye!"

I took my leave. By the time I reached the door, the kindly server was already standing there, ready to open it for me.

"Dzienkuje," I said to him. *"Do widzenia."* (Goodbye.)

"Do zobacienia, Pani, do zobacienia!" (Until we meet again, Madame. Until we meet again!) He stood in the doorway waving until I'd turned the corner onto the main road, and was out of sight.

EPILOGUE *I never had occasion to travel back to Gdansk on the Baltic seacoast, but I never forgot the kind-hearted server, and the nuclear family who were so happy at a time when I was feeling so blue. Yes, when I'm in a better mood, perhaps I'll return. I really don't like* *myself when I'm depressed. I'm really not good company at all. Actually, now that I think back, I've never had a spell of depression since then.*

Perhaps it's because at home, I always have something to do: read the morning paper, answer correspondence, take my daily walk to the post office to mail one of my books or a letter to a friend, ride my stationary bike, answer my e-mail, tidy up my apartment, visit my dear children/neighbors/friends, watch my favorite TV programs, write a celebratory poem for my family or friends.

Or, maybe, another true short story.

14

**THREE-YEAR-OLD GORDON'S
BIRTHDAY PARADE**
Seattle, Washington 1994

PROLOGUE *Today was my first grandson Gordon's birthday. He was three years old, and could indicate his age by holding up the correct number of fingers on one hand. Yes, he was ready for his birthday.*

Today, his mother said he was big enough to wear his new Viking suit. He first put on his regular pants and turtleneck shirt, and his mother tied his shoes. Then she helped him buckle on the molded plastic breastplate, pewter-gray in color, the same as his helmet and sword. They all came in a packet last Christmas from the Smithsonian Museum, where his Auntie Hikmet worked.

He practiced pulling the sword out of its sheath and looked at himself in the mirror. A Viking! He looked like the warrior in his storybook.

Yes, he was ready for his parade, his very own parade. His mother said she didn't like the idea of taking all the children on the block to the Chucky Cheese place. Or to the Bumper Car place. It was "a budget matter," she said. So, instead, he was going to have a "real Parade!"

She had gotten up early in the morning to make pink lemonade, and to bake and ice cupcakes, enough for a large crowd. Now, she was ready. She glanced at the clock on the mantel and said, "It's time to start!"

The Saturday morning was clear and sunny, the sky was blue, the little birds were singing in "Old Pink," the big cherry tree in front of the house. Gordon picked up his sword, and marched out to the wooden gate where his mother, Melike, stood waiting.

A wicker basket by the gate held a motley collection of long silk scarves, hats, and caps. The large carton next to it held sparkly magic wands, an assortment of small percussion instruments, and other odd paraphernalia. Melike picked up a toy bugle from the percussion box and signaled to Gordon. "I think I see someone coming to the Parade!" she announced as the Bugler, and blew three short notes on the bugle: *Tah! Tah! Tah!*

A young mother with several small children was already walking up the street, shouting, "Happy Birthday, Gordon!" Doors along the tree-lined street opened and children ran out to join the gathering throng. The Bugler attracted the children like the magical Pied Piper of Hamlin Town in the storybook; they all clustered around the Bugler, who was handing out things.

For each child, she reached into the basket for something to put on the head: a bright cap, a straw hat, a striped silk scarf to wind into a turban. Then she reached in the carton for something to carry in the hand: a sparkling wand, a piccolo, a cymbal, or a tambourine.

Out of a fresh package, she pulled small but loud Happy New Year's noisemakers. When every child was outfitted, she put her toy bugle in her pocket, took a small snare drum from the carton, and rummaged around for the drumsticks.

Gordon's tall Cousin Jee-Joe from Turkey, who had promised to take pictures on the camcorder, was not yet in sight, but there was no holding back the excited throng. It was Time to March!

Now the Melike the Bugler became the Melike the Drummer, and she rapped out a snappy *Tat-ah-tat-tat! Tat-ah-tat-tat!* on her little drum.

The Drummer starts off the parade, with one little boy and his mother.

To the accompanying mothers, the Drummer announced: "We'll go down to the corner, cross our street, go up the other side of our street to the end, turn left one block up the hill, go west on the street by the church, turn left, and down left at the next corner, then back home again. We'll cover a large square in approximately an hour. Hooray!"

All the children milling about echoed: "Hooray! Hooray!" The Drummer helped the boys adjust their funny caps and magicians' hats, and roll up their turbans. She tied the girls' colorfully floating scarves. They all lined up behind the Gordon, the Viking Leader.

129

Melike, the Drummer, calls the children to follow.

Gordon and Auntie Shanti

Gordon's grandmother joins in with her noisemaker.

"All right, everybody! We're off to see the Wizard, the Wonderful Wizard of Oz!" sang the Drummer, rapping out the rhythm on her tin drum. At her signal, there was a clashing of cymbals, a jingling of tambourines, and shrill little pipe squeaks — creating a wild burst of cacophonous sound that merged with the little children's happy voices.

Urged on by their mothers, whoever was old enough to know words to a song, sang at the top of their sweet voices. This initial outburst of energy quickly burnt itself out, naturally, and the children settled down to walking or skipping along, occasionally shaking their music-makers.

By now the throng stretched out by the dozens, and included accompanying parents with babies in strollers and small children on tricycles. It extended half a block down the street.. Walking west to the corner, the crowd crossed the little street and turned back eastward again, to avoid a construction project in progress at the far end of the block.

By this time, Cousin Jee-Joe hove into view, shouting "Wait! Wait!" His bus was late, he said apologetically, and he had to run up the hill to catch up with the Parade. Now, as the Camcorder of the Parade, Cousin Jee-Joe began taking pictures from the back of the line, and from many angles. He was the busiest Marcher of all.

Little Gordon, at the head of the line with Auntie Shanti, had already reached the house of the neighborhood St. Bernard dog. The dog's sensitive ears perked up at the unusual noise, and it bounded out onto the sidewalk to look at the lively children with their bright caps and hats, and scarves fluttering in the breeze. The enormous dog's appearance effectively stopped the Parade.

At the sight of this creature more than twice his size, little Gordon was naturally startled. Rather than screaming, crying, or running away to his mother, Gordon's instinctive reaction was to stand, draw, and thrust his small plastic sword in the approximate direction of the dog. *(Since the three-year-old's TV viewing was limited to non-violent "Teletubbies" programs, it can only be assumed that this reaction was not learned from television, but instinctive. How else? Perhaps from his picture book?)*

Hearing the shouts of the little Paraders out on the sidewalk, the lady of the house stepped out to take a look. She ordered the St. Bernard back inside his house, apologized sweetly and waved to the children.

Forward and onward, the straggly line of frolicking kids moved on to the street corner, now congested by a large crowd and a conglomeration of moving vans, trucks, and other vehicles parked in front.

A crew of men and women — all wearing hardhats and moving about actively in the front yard — could be seen toting bags of concrete, sawing long pieces of lumber, hammering and nailing boards together.

This dynamic spectacle was enough to totally halt the whole procession of birthday celebrants — children and adults.

For the benefit of the children, one of the front-line marching mothers read aloud the large sign posted on the sidewalk:

> **HABITAT for HUMANITY**
> *Building Homes for the Homeless*

Simultaneously, both groups stopped in their tracks to take note of each other: the hard-working volunteers on the lawn, and the little Paraders on the opposite sidewalk.

"What's going on today?" asked the foreman-looking man carrying a large notebook in one hand and a measuring tape in the other.

"We're having a Birthday Parade. My son is three years old today!" said the Drummer, proudly pointing out Gordon, then added, "I see you're building a house! Good luck to you!"

"Good luck!" echoed the accompanying mothers nearby.

"Okay, kids, let's all say Good luck and Goodbye!" She rapped on her drum and gave the marching signal.

"Good luck! Goodbye!" echoed the little ones, most reluctant to leave the fascinating scene. Their eyes were glued to the crew of strong men and women poised at this very moment to raise the roof into place, shouting directions as they stooped and lifted.

Obedient to the insistent beat of the Drummer, the children turned left, slowly moving ahead up the short block, and turning left again at the next corner, following the Drummer westward.

"*Rat-a-tat-tat!*" went the tiny tin drum, with the percussionists following the beat to the best of their ability. At the clangor and happy children's shouts, windows and house doors opened all along the quiet street; heads stuck out and people emerged to see what on Earth was going on. Although they'd never seen a colorful spectacle like this in their neighborhood, it didn't take them long to figure out it was a children's parade of some kind, and they caught the spirit instantaneously. "Hi! Hey! Hooray! Happy Birthday!" came the neighborly shouts. Some people stepped outside to get a better view and satisfy their curiosity.

"Are you going to have a really *big* birthday cake?" asked one curious grandfather, digging away in his rock garden.

132

"No," answered the Drummer. "We're going to have treats! Lots and lots of treats! And lemonade in our garden! Hooray! Hooray!"

"Hooray!" repeated little Gordon, echoing his mother and adding, "Lemonade and *treats!*"

The procession made their way past the row of pretty houses with their well-groomed shrubbery, each patch of landscape as different as the owner's fancy could imagine, but blending somehow into the neighborhood's overall charming appearance.

By now, the Drummer had guided her straggly parade to the church corner and turned left, down the short hill to the corner. "Hey! There's *my* house!" yelled sharp-eyed little Gordon when he got to the bottom of the hill. "Hey!" he yelled again, *"Treats!"* and picked up speed.

The Drummer picked up speed herself, to welcome the crowd arriving in her little garden. She signaled a welcome to come in the gate, *"Rat - a - tat- tat! Rat - a - tat- tat!"*

There, on an extra long, low table were stacks of folded paper napkins, and rows of large, covered trays filled with freshly frosted cupcakes. Pitchers of cold lemonade and cartons of paper cups sat waiting on a side table.

Some of the accompanying mothers organized a potty-break line that followed the cobblestone path around through the back garden, with an entrance to the downstairs bathroom. When the large crowd had gathered in the front garden and was overflowing onto the sidewalk outside the gate, Melike put her drum in the box and picked up one tray of cupcakes. With a flourish, she presented the first one to the Birthday Boy. Several mothers followed suit, passing the cupcakes around to all the paraders to pick their favorite color: snow white, peach pink, chocolate brown, lime green.

Other mothers poured out cups of lemonade for the thirsty crowd of children and adults sitting on the porch, the steps, the grass, the cool cobblestone path around the house, or out on the parking strip in the shade of the big cherry tree.

Melike lit the three candles on the Birthday Boy's cupcake and shouted, "Happy Birthday, Gordon!" as he blew out his candles. The crowd picked up on the Birthday Song, and joined in. Some children sang so enthusiastically they needed a second cupcake and lots of lemonade, because they were so thirsty. Even Cousin Jee-Jo needed several extra cupcakes because he had run so fast up the hill to catch up with the Parade. He finished taking pictures and put his camcorder into its bag. Now it looked like it was near the end of the Parade, and time for a speech from the Birthday Boy's mom.

"Well, boys and girls, did you enjoy the Parade?" she asked the happy crowd. A shout went up, and grew in volume as the ones out of earshot caught on. "Hooray! Hooray!" they all shouted.

"Thank you all for coming! It was the best children's parade I ever saw, so I thank you again! And please have a cupcake to take home! Hooray!"

At the last cheery shout, she picked up the wicker basket to collect the scarves and headgear, and brought out the carton for the percussion instruments. As they made their way out to the street, the children dutifully removed their headgear and dropped it into the basket, dropped their instruments into the carton at the gate, and dropped their cupcake papers and napkins in the trash box.

"Good bye, Gordon," said some. "Thank you for the parade, Gordon," said others. "Happy Birthday, Gordon," said the mothers as they guided their children's tricycles out of the garden, and pushed the baby strollers onto the sidewalk.

The Paraders walk to the treats in the garden.

EPILOGUE *The magical atmosphere of the Parade had disappeared, but we Readers can imagine that many a small Parader dreamed of wearing a hat and marching along to the beat of the small tin drum.*

There was tall Cousin Jee-Joe, running to catch up with the Parade. Rat - a - tat- tat! There was the Birthday Boy in his Viking suit. Rat - a - tat- tat! There were the strong workers, all lifting the roof onto the new house. HABITAT for HUMANITY! Rat - a - tat- tat! There were the neighbors on the next street, waving and cheering as the Parade went by. Rat - a - tat- tat! Yes, Gordon, it was truly a real Parade! Hooray! Hooray! Happy Birthday!

134

15

GORDON *at the* DOLL FESTIVAL
Mukogawa Fort Wright Institute, Spokane WA 1999

PROLOGUE *In 1990, I retired from the Foreign Service and moved back to my hometown of Spokane, Washington. After several years of quiet life in the countryside, I was enticed into teaching English at the nearby women's college for Japanese students, Mukogawa Fort Wright Institute. The students came from their home institute in Nishinomiya, Spokane's sister city in Japan.*

The next ten years or so was to prove exciting and culturally enriching. In teaching Japanese students about my country and culture, I learned much about Japanese customs and traditions.

As a child, I had learned about Kite Day or Boys' Day, held in Japan on May 5 — the fifth day of the fifth month of the year. Young boys celebrated this special day with kite-making activities and competitions. A traditional symbol painted on the paper kites is the koi or carp fish, a symbol of strength and courage. Carp kites are attached to flag poles to mark the advent of Boys' Day. Today, it is called "Children's Day," and boys and girls celebrate it together.

Now, at Mukogawa Fort Wright Institute in Spokane, I was learning about the annual Hina Matsuri (Doll Festival) celebrated by girls on March 3 — the third day of the third month of the year.

On this day, the girls put on their special kimonos, and take out their treasured dolls that have been put away since the previous year. These dolls are not toys, but rather, traditional symbols of ideal Japanese womanhood, passed down from mother to daughter, from one generation to the next, and so on. The young girls in every house arrange the dolls in their special order: the Emperor and Empress on the highest tier, members of the royal court on the level below, and beneath them, other dolls of lesser rank. Special mochi balls (sweets made of bean paste) and other treats are placed as offerings in ceremonial arrangements in front of the dolls. The young girls sing special little songs, dance ceremonial dances, play special music on a wooden flute, or on a koto (a kind of large zither or horizontal harp with 13 silk strings).

At the end of the day's celebrations, the dolls are carefully removed from their positions of honor, wrapped in special tissue, and placed back into their boxes, where they will rest until the next year's Hina Matsuri. This must all be done before the sun sets, else it will bring bad luck to the young girl. (Perhaps she will never marry; or if she does, perhaps she will never have a child.) The Hina Matsuri traditions have many delicate details.

The lovely tradition of *Hina Matsuri* (Doll Festival) is celebrated more or less at Mukogawa Fort Wright Institute (MFWI) in Spokane, Washington as it is celebrated in Japan. Now, it is also shared with many American school children, not only in the Spokane area, but in the wider Pacific Northwest and other cities across the United States, through MFWI's Outreach Program.

Since the founding of this women's college in 1980, MFWI has invited children from elementary schools in Spokane and neighboring towns that have graciously invited the Mukogawa students to visit their schools. Gradually the number of schools interested in Japanese culture and customs has grown to include institutes as far away as the East Coast.

The American children who are invited to Spokane have been practicing various Japanese songs and other activities as part of their geography and world cultures classes, and their participation in the Doll Festival provides a delightful counterpart to the Japanese girls' exquisitely colorful kimonos, artwork, dances, and music.

It is a special privilege to attend one of MFWI's *Hina Matsuri* [Doll Festival] celebrations. Here, American schoolchildren meet their 'Neighbors across the Pacific,' as Mrs. Michiko Takaoka, the first director of the Cultural Center, always liked to point out. Mrs. Takaoka had kindly sent invitations to my grandson Gordon, who was chosen as a representative of his elementary school in Seattle to receive a Friendship Doll for his school. As a former MFWI faculty member, I was also invited, along with Gordon's mother, Melike, who drove us from Seattle across the Cascade Mountains to Spokane.

Up until an hour before we were scheduled to appear in the auditorium, eight-year-old Gordon had flatly refused to dress up for the occasion. He insisted on wearing his school clothes (old blue jeans and tee shirt), and absolutely refused to wear his best jacket and trousers, or his white shirt and tie. I think the idea of wearing a suit made him nervous, and probably the whole prospect of appearing on stage was making him more and more stubborn.

Gordon's mother (Melike) and I used all our powers of persuasion to get the little boy to change his mind. We tried to impress on him the formality of the ceremony, and the fact that the men in the group on stage would all be wearing ties. Gordon would be standing, I explained, next to one of the most famous doll makers in Japan, Shosuko Genga *sensei*. As a Master Doll Maker, he would be the honored guest, and would be wearing his best ceremonial clothes for the occasion, as well as a special hairdo with ivory chopsticks skewering his topknot in place. Gordon was too young to be able to visualize any doll maker, let alone one dressed in Japanese ceremonial clothing. I could well understand this; the elegant artist who appeared that day, outfitted in all his traditional costume, had to be seen in person to be appreciated. He was a strikingly handsome figure of a man!

But to persuade Gordon to put on his suit, his mother and I desperately tried all kinds of bribery. We promised he could have his favorite dessert for dinner at his favorite restaurant in town, and he could visit his favorite uncle's farm nearby to feed his favorite black-and-white cow. At this point, Gordon gave in halfway, agreeing to wear a white shirt, his striped tie, and his best pants — but *no* jacket! This was the best we could hope for, and we accepted the compromise.

Although Gordon was quiet but extremely nervous, he slipped into his fresh clothes quickly and allowed his mother to knot his tie; then we three rushed to the auditorium across campus, with minutes to spare. The groups of Mukogawa students were filing in as we entered; the visiting American schoolchildren who would also be performing were already seated in the front side section. A few front row seats for the visiting dignitaries sat empty, waiting for the formal opening of the program.

Mrs. Takaoka, exquisitely lovely in a flowered silk kimono, welcomed us backstage, introduced us to the smartly dressed Japanese Counsel from Seattle, and to the handsomely attired Master Doll Maker from Osaka, Shosuko Genga *sensei.* Melike had slipped into a seat at the back of the room where she could get a good view of the full stage and take photos.

Quietly, Mrs. Takaoka demonstrated to Gordon how he should hold the doll when it was presented to him for his school. He was to say "Thank you" loudly enough for the audience to hear, and hold the doll until an assistant came to take it from him.

We others were to follow Mrs. Takaoka out on stage, bow a little, and stand while she introduced us individually, and while she presented the Friendship Doll to Gordon for his school. Her assistant would come on stage, bow a little, and take the doll from Gordon and exit the stage. Back in the Cultural Center, she would put on special gloves, wrap the doll in a special cloth, and place it in a special box for its journey to Gordon's school **TOPS** *(The **O**ptions **P**rogram **S**chool),* in Seattle. Then at Mrs. Takaoka's signal, we should all leave the stage and take seats in the front row. On cue, we followed Mrs. Takaoka's precise instructions on exiting the stage, took our seats in the front row, and the main program began.

Everything in the Doll Festival that day went off smoothly as planned. Once seated with the audience, we were able to watch all the well-rehearsed dances, songs, and marital arts demonstrations by the Mukogawa students, and all the sweet Japanese songs and activities learned and performed by the visiting American schoolchildren.

There was lots of applause from all sides for all the performances. It was a happy, festive celebration, with the pretty 'Miss Tokushima' Friendship Doll in her glass case, standing on a pedestal of honor to preside over the festivities. *(Each year, 'Miss Tokushima' was formally borrowed from the Cheney Cowles Museum of Spokane for the Doll Festival. She was then carefully re-wrapped by a gloved attendant, and returned to her stand in the Museum until the next year's Hina matsuri.)*

A multitude of other beloved dolls of all kinds — Raggedy Anns, Barbies, Dolly Dimples — sat in rows on the side stage, adding color and an American dimension to the Doll Festival. The American dolls would be retrieved by their young American owners at the end of their visit to the celebration.

Just before the end of the program, Mrs. Takaoka requested our presence on stage; the photographer was ready to take pictures. Gordon was asked to stand next to Master Doll Maker Shosuko Genga *sensei* in his traditionally styled brocade jacket, black trousers, white cotton one-toed socks and sandals. He looked like a colorful fashion plate come to life from a long-ago period in Japanese history, with his jet-black hair combed back to a glistening sleekness and skewered into a topknot by a carved ivory hair ornament. The beautifully soft pastel flowers of Mrs. Takaoka's silk kimono seemed to pale in comparison next to the artist's magnificently handsome attire!

It is my sincere honor to greet the Honorable Fumiko Saiga, Consul General of Japan, Seattle; Rikio Minamiyama, Consul; John Powers, Spokane Mayor; Gary Livingston, Superintendent, Spokane School District 81; Yvonne Morton and Ann Price from the Northwest Museum of Arts and Culture, formally Cheney Cowles Museum. I am especially pleased to welcome our guests from Massachusetts, Melinda Willis and Pat Kenneally; from Tennessee, Mary Smath; a group from Seattle, Hironi Pingry, Anna Maria Malkoc, a former faculty member, her daughter Eden Malkoc and grandson Gordon Loop; and last but not least, Mr. Shosuke Genga, renown master doll artist, and his daughter, Yoko Kawamura from Osaka Japan. Welcome to all these distinguished guests and everyone.

My special thanks to Mr. Haralam and his students for telling the Friendship Doll story in such a wonderful way.

Hina Matsuri, has more than 1,000 years of history giving the message for young girls' happiness. Originating as a family tradition, *Hina* dolls are displayed in homes and handed down from mother to daughter for generations.

These days, *Hina* doll sets are also displayed at schools, hotels, and department stores, and everywhere in Japan during the month of March. Girls often put their favorite dolls on tiers at home to share the joy. Even now, some 1927 American Friendship dolls are displayed with *Hina* Dolls sets in some elementary schools in Japan.

The symbol of *Hina Matsuri* is peach flowers. *Hina* dolls are reminders of family history: of grandma, grandpa, of mother's cooking, happy childhood and of friends. Additionally, March is the time of change in Japan.

Graduations are held in March and a new school year begins in April. Springtime is the season and *hina* dolls send feelings of new beginnings and growth.

Now let me introduce you to Miss Tokushima, a very quiet smiling lady. She was born in Tokyo in 1927. She is 74 years old. She looks so young for her age.

Miss Tokushima and her 57 sister dolls are top class artistic dolls who came to the US as dolls of friendship. Miss Tokushima and all the Friendship dolls in both countries are witnesses to the long history of US-Japan relations. It was early in 1992 when I first saw her at then Cheney Cowles. I was overwhelmed by her innocent smile and clear beauty. Immediately, I decided to celebrate the Doll Festival with her in Spokane. We were motivated to show our appreciation to the people of Spokane for their long protection of the doll, and secondly, we wanted to share the history and story of friendship between the U.S. and Japan.

We celebrated the first Doll Festival on March 3, 1992 at Cheney Cowles Museum. Since then, she has been attending the celebration every year and has a special impact on us. We appreciate the generosity of the Northwest Museum of Arts and Culture, formally Cheney Cowles, to show Miss Tokushima to the public.

Dr. Sidney Gulick III, grandson of the initiator, and his wife Frances, continue the noble vision of Dr. Gulick. Both doctors of mathematics at the University of Maryland, the Gulicks have sent over 100 American dolls with hand-made clothes to Japan. They remain very active in promoting friendship and international relations, as did their grandfather.

Michiko, Hironi Pingry, Michiko, Genga, center, Gordon Loop, Anna Maria Malkoc, Consul General Saiga, Ed Tsutakawa, and doll given to Tajo Sei, Seattle

Mukogawa Fort Wright Institute newsletter, 1999
Gordon Loop, center, holding Friendship Doll for his school
[The doll was made by master doll maker Shosuko Genga sensei, standing next to Gordon.]

Like watchful big sisters, the Mukogawa students escorted the visiting elementary-school children to seats in the spacious dining room, where everyone was served a *bento (obento)* box for lunch, including a pair of chopsticks, and a fork, in case they were unaccustomed to chopsticks.

Although Gordon had balked at wearing his best suit for the program, he did not balk at the *bento* lunch box. By the age of three, he had already developed a taste for a number of exotic foods: sushi, cold noodles, shrimp-fried rice, broccoli, smoked oysters, and of course, *mochi* balls. Now at the age of eight, he was more than ready to try everything in his bento box. He savored every bite of the delicious treats, and he used his chopsticks.

On their return drive home to Seattle late that afternoon, Gordon totally relaxed in the back seat. As instructed, he had received — and turned over to the Cultural Center assistant — the precious Japanese Friendship Doll, now wrapped snugly and riding safely in the trunk of their car. He was proud to have carried out his responsibility on stage: he had met the Master Doll Maker, they had bowed to each other, and he had eaten a delicious bento lunch served by a beautiful student from Japan, who had given him extra treats. With eyes drooping and head nestled into his favorite car pillow, he sighed contentedly: "That was the most fun I ever had, Mom!"

EPILOGUE   Although Gordon did not realize it at the moment, his duties as TOPS Elementary School representative were not yet over. The following week, Melike telephoned to make arrangements with the principal of TOPS where Gordon was a third grader. It was decided that Gordon should formally present the Friendship Doll to the school on the forthcoming International Night.

On this International evening, many parents from other countries agreed to wear their native dress, and bring special dishes from their regions for everyone to taste. The celebration was always held in the gym that also served as the school auditorium, as it had a raised stage. Many long tables were lined up in readiness to hold the banquet of food; early guests carried in the folding chairs and set them at the tables, others lined up to sample the many exotic dishes, carefully labeled with name of the dish and country of origin.

It was an amazing display of food from around the world, and equally exciting to get a close-up view of the colorful clothing worn in faraway regions that we stay-at-homes usually see only on the pages of "National Geographic."

Families introduced themselves, mingled, and savored the exotic food; altogether, it was a delicious and educational introduction to the evening's program.

For the Friendship Doll presentation, Gordon and I had rehearsed what we were going to say: I would introduce a history of the Friendship Doll as briefly as I could, and then Mr. Tubbs, the school principal, would escort Gordon carrying the doll onto the stage and introduce him to the audience. So that was how it worked out.

Gordon, wearing fresh school pants, freshly ironed white shirt and striped tie, looked neat and serious holding the Friendship Doll by its mahogany stand. He held it carefully so the audience could see the beautiful red and gold brocade kimono, the white silk obi (sash) around its waist, its exquisitely painted porcelain face, and its jet-black hair in a special hairdo.

Speaking directly and clearly to the Principal, Gordon said: "This is a Friendship Doll from Japan. It was given to the TOPS Elementary School in Seattle by the Mukogawa Institute of Japan, in the interest of friendship and world peace."

Mr. Tubbs accepted the Friendship Doll, thanked Gordon for representing TOPS Elementary School at the Doll Festival in Spokane, and told the audience the Japanese Friendship Doll would have a place of honor in TOPS Exhibit Hall.

Friendship Doll Bookmark

The Friendship Doll

I stand so still;
my lips don't move
and yet I sing
of peace and love.

Your ears can't hear
my melody,
the song I bring
from across the sea.

But hearts will hear
the song I bring,
if they are quiet,
and listening.

*Anna-Maria Malkoç
Hina Matsuri Doll Festival
MFWI Spokane 3/01/01*

(Try a Google search for Japanese Friendship Dolls, in Wikipedia.)

16

PLAYTIME *with* LITTLE DYLAN
Mukilteo, Washington ...2000

PROLOGUE *My second grandson, Dylan Sharief Malkoç, was born in Mukilteo, Washington on October 29, 1997.*

Dark-haired and blue-eyed, healthy and active, Dylan was welcomed by all our extended family. As his paternal grandmother, I was eager to find signs of family resemblances to his father Timur.

Also to his Turkish grandfather Malkoç, or to his Iraqi grandfather Sharief, both of whom, sadly, had passed away some years before. But so far as I could see, Baby Dylan exhibited no unexpected family characteristics. He was, simply, a bright and handsome blend of his paternal and maternal ancestors.

As happy as I was in those days, I often thought I'd have been even happier if I weren't living so far from my daughters Hikmet (in Washington DC), Kamuran (in Everett), and Melike (in Seattle); also from my son Timur in Mukilteo, and now, my two grandsons, Gordon and Dylan. With the exception of eldest daughter Hikmet working at the time in the Smithsonian Museum in Washington DC, they were all located in the Puget (Pew-jet) Sound area, each within an hour's drive from Seattle. They were all putting pressure on me to leave Spokane and move nearer to Seattle.

At the time Dylan was born, I was retired and living in my parents' old family house just outside Spokane, 300 miles east of Seattle. In order to visit my grandsons and grown children, I had to make various arrangements to travel by car or Greyhound bus. (Train schedules that picked up Spokane passengers at one o'clock in the morning were absolutely out for me.) My children all complained about the tiresome trip across the Cascades, and urged me to move to the Seattle area.

At the same time, other factors were affecting my pleasant, orderly life: arthritic knees at home, at school, and in the garden. Keeping up the house became more of a burden, and I began to consider making some drastic changes in my life to accommodate these issues.

I dearly wished one of my children would take over the family house. When none of them were interested in living in it, that settled it for me. As heartbreaking as it was, I retired from my beloved school, sold the family house, and moved to Timur and Paige's place in Mukilteo.

Timur was having the lower-level rooms adapted into a comfortable apartment with French doors that opened onto a green lawn and small garden, and a panorama of Puget Sound not far down the hill. On sunny days, I would be able to work outside on my writing

144

projects. Inside, I would have the privacy I needed to concentrate on my stories, while still being close to my son and his family.

When Hikmet moved from Washington DC, to live in Edmonds, I was overjoyed now that my family was together once again — or, at least in the same region. We had been separated during the many years I worked in faraway Turkey and Poland, and then in Spokane, Washington on the other side of the Cascades.

Every day was a challenge in adjusting to my new environment; every day was a new learning experience. I was living in my son's home where I had playtime with grandson Baby Dylan every day; by this time, he was going on two, and was able to toddle. I could see my son, three daughters, and grandson Gordon often. My heart was full.

At the early age of 18 months or so, Paige had already scheduled Dylan for swimming classes at the YMCA pool to get him used to the water, and then to the basics of swimming. To his parents' delight — and relief, Dylan took to swimming like a duck to water; swimming is an essential life skill for anyone living near boats and water. Also, it's a necessary skill for any child whose Great-Grandfather has a summer house in Hawaii and invites him to come swimming in the glorious blue waters of the south Pacific.

As a reward for doing well in his swimming lessons, Dylan was signed up for a "swimming experience with tame dolphins" at a Hawaiian resort hotel. The young swimmer returned with many impressive photographs, and a new appreciation of not only about dolphins but a wide variety of sea creatures. Although he hadn't learned to read yet, he informed us of numerous facts: coral reefs should be protected, for instance, because all coral is living, a fact I hadn't thought about before.

Back on the Mainland in Mukilteo, my playtime with Dylan was now scheduled along with his swimming lessons, kindergarten, and sometimes softball practice with Papa after work. This left an hour or two mid-morning, before lunch and nap, when Dylan and I could play together inside or outside, weather depending.

Over the course of several years, we had well-established communication routines.

One morning, I remember awaking to sounds coming from the bedroom overhead that were clearly distinguishable in the early Mukilteo air. I recognized Mozart's simple melody that American children sing to "Twinkle, Twinkle, Little Star."

It was not coming from the radio, I soon realized, but from Dylan's crib upstairs. The little two-year-old was singing to himself: *"A-b-c-d-e-f-g, h-i-j-k-l-m-n-o-p . . . ."* He must have learned it at Play School that week.

I was mesmerized, listening to his sweet little voice as he sang every note, clear and true, over and over. And, he was actually carrying a tune! This was a thrilling discovery for me, as not everyone in the family *could* carry a tune, including Dylan's mother and my very own mother.

From that morning on, I watched and listened for signs of Dylan's musical inclinations. Once, when he was about three, I saw him slow down as he walked through the living room, past the stereo that he was never allowed to touch. It was playing a CD recording of a melodious and soulful cello sonata. He paused a moment.

"Oh! *That* was a nice tone!" he commented aloud to no one in particular. Then he went outside to play bat-the-ball in the garden.

As far as I knew, apart from little group songs in the classrooms, the children in Dylan's Play School or in his Preschool did not have music classes. Some children had private piano or violin lessons after school, but the only music Dylan listened to on a regular basis was Timur's guitar playing. Every night at bedtime, Timur would tuck Dylan in bed, then take out his guitar, tune it, and strum a few chords. In his soothing baritone, he would sing the words of old Beatles' favorites from the seventies. Little Dylan would sing along with Timur whenever he knew a few words, and happily drift off to sleep listening to his father's music.

During the week, Timur worked long hours, usually leaving Paige in the house before Dylan woke up, and sometimes not returning from work until Dylan's bedtime. So this lullaby hour was a precious time in the family.

As soon as Dylan had mastered walking, about the age of two as I recall, he had learned to crawl backward, down the soft, carpeted stairs, then stand up, and knock on my apartment door. My apartment held great fascination for him; it was full of books and unusual little toys, and the door was always closed.

Every morning, he needed to ask permission from his mother to visit me, and he needed to knock on the door before he could come in. "Oh! Is there someone knocking at my *door?"* I would call out, and the tiny knock would be repeated. "Oh! I wonder who it is!" I would say to myself loudly, waiting a moment or two for suspense to build — but not too much — before opening the door.

We would repeat some version of this little scenario every morning after Dylan had gotten permission from his mother to come visiting, usually with a little race car or some other toy in hand to play with. He and I had favorite games for which he would make up rules as he went along; one long-time favorite was "Race Car." This game involved selecting a matchbox-sized racecar from Dylan's toy box.

The cars had to be pushed off to a good start so they would go around inside the rim of the big Turkish-copper tray that served as my end table. The tray's rounded-up edge prevented the tiny metal toys from flying off; they would go round and round the rim until they ran out of man-power. The game provided us endless pleasure, as the rules were elastic, and depended entirely on Dylan's whimsy of the moment.

Dylan the Cowboy on a real pony, wearing a bright blue cowboy hat

Gradually, as Dylan's vocabulary developed, the scenarios at the door became actual dialogues, with Dylan responding in words and then phrases and whole sentences. Occasionally, there were some mornings when there was no verbal response after the first timid knock, and the knock might be repeated several times. This meant that the appropriate response was as yet beyond his vocabulary level. The morning, for instance, when I opened the door to behold a miniature Batman, attired in crimson cape and blue playsuit, standing motionless in the doorway, in a breathless pose.

"Oh! Look everybody! It's *Batman!* Wow!" I would

exclaim, applauding vigorously. "Turn around, Batman, let's see your cape swirl!" I would hum a bit of Batman's intro music to set the scene.

As Baby Batman would obediently turn and swirl, I would applaud even more vigorously, then escort him to the mirror to see the full effect for himself. It was the swirling cape, I think, that made the Batman costume such a long-lasting favorite, until it finally wore out.

The Buzz Lightyear costume was another of the many dramatic outfits inherited from his Cousin Gordon, who had long ago outgrown them. This space-age costume was all shining silver, from moon boots to cape and helmet. As I recall, it also came with a "light" sword that had cosmic powers when illuminated: it vanquished the enemy on the spot.

"Wow! *Buzz Lightyear!* Wow!" I exclaimed after I recognized the tiny figure holding his space-travel pose. I was moved to applaud wildly. "Buzz Lightyear! *Bla-a-a-ast off*!" And the miniature space hero would jab his light sword in karate chops at an invisible space foe.

For me, a retired English teacher, every day brought fascinating evidence of Dylan's rapid linguistic development — as well as his knowledge of the popular comic book/TV heroes of the day.

One morning, following doctor's orders, I was resting on the day bed after my daily knee-replacement exercises, when I heard a sharp tap at the door. Who else could it be but Dylan?

The door had no peephole to view visitors, so I called out as usual: "Who is it?"

"It's Dylan!" came the self-assured little four-year-old voice.

"Oh," I responded, "in that case, *please*, do come in!" and I stepped carefully over to the door, pushing my cane aside as I did so. "Hug first!" I reminded him, and took note of how tall he was that day: Nearly up to my elbow. I kissed the top of his head, and sat down.

EPILOGUE I can still envision the scene that morning as clearly as if it had been filmed in Disneyland.

Sharp-eyed Dylan looked around, as he always did, to take note of anything new or unusual in the apartment in the past few weeks, while he was away visiting his other grandmother, and his great-grandfather in Oregon. During that time, I'd had knee surgery to replace my bad right knee, spent a week in the hospital, another in rehab, and was now settling into a routine of rest and knee exercises. Dylan immediately spotted my hospital cane with the adjustable holes, and picked it up.

"What's this, Baba Anne?" (I had asked him to call me "Father's Mother," which means paternal grandmother in Turkish, as a way of distinguishing me from his maternal grandmother Jacquie and his great-grandmother Madeline. It is also to honor his deceased grandfather Selahattin's Turkish heritage.)

Before I could even begin to explain about the metal cane, Dylan had raised it to his lips as if it were a long flute, and began to blow on the first hole while fingering closed the other holes.

Spontaneously, and simultaneously without missing a beat, I began to whistle "Yankee Doodle" while Dylan marched forward to my music. When he reached the far end of the daybed, he did a quick double step to round the corner and raised the cane with both hands high above his head, like the drum major's baton he'd seen at the last Fourth of July parade. He continued to strut back and forth around the room until I was breathless from whistling, and we both collapsed in laughter.

"Yes, Dylan," I told him, "you really do have music in you. It's a gift!" And we celebrated our spontaneous little parade with small glasses of grape juice, sipping delicately from bendable straws.

17

LITTLE MILES, *the* "SOCCER STRATEGIST"
Mukilteo, Washington 2005

PROLOGUE *My third grandson, Miles Jonathan Malkoç, was born in Mukilteo, Washington on January 6, 2001. As I did with my first two grandsons, I looked for similarities and signs of family traits. "Babies' personality traits show up even when they're very young," a wise old nurse had once told me.*

Although I made a conscientious effort to avoid comparing my grandsons judgmentally, I could see that like his four-year-old brother Dylan, baby Miles was a blend of both his father's and his mother's looks: blue-eyed and brown-haired. Unlike his active brother, however, he seemed quieter, and more content to cuddle on someone's lap and observe what was going on around him.

Before Miles was born, his maternal great-grandmother Madeleine had made a small white and yellow blanket in anticipation, and all during his infancy it lay atop the crib he was tucked into each night. He became attached to this soft little blanket, to the point that he cried for it when it was missing, and would not be appeased until it was found and tucked over him. He would rub a corner of the blanket between his tiny thumb and forefinger until he fell asleep each night.

I had read about babies feeling attached to "comfort blankets," but in my busy family I had never seen such a bonding until Miles came along. That crib blanket had to go with him everywhere, all the months of his infancy. It needed frequent washing because of its overuse, but could be washed only while he was asleep. As a result, the synthetic texture of the originally soft nylon turned harsh to the touch; in addition, a large hole formed in the middle. I could see the hole growing larger, and a number of times I volunteered to sew it up, but Miles never allowed me to touch it.

It was one afternoon while he was napping in my apartment that I got up the nerve to mend it. When he woke up, I showed him the precious blanket: it was all mended, and the hole was gone. He looked it over suspiciously, and then nodded a small smile of acceptance.

Some months earlier, he had given up his pacifier, which, along with his crib blanket, had soothed him to sleep each night. No amount of persuasion from his father or mother had moved him to quit the pacifier. It was not until his brother Dylan told him that he'd be going to playschool soon, and the kids there didn't take their pacifiers with them. "Only the babies have pacifiers," declared brother Dylan. So that was the end of the pacifier for Miles.

But Miles was still clinging to his blanket — until the morning that he forgot it at home. "Papa!" he exclaimed, after his father had backed out of the tricky driveway and was maneuvering the sloping curve at the top of the road, "Papa, I forgot my blanket!"

152

"What shall we do, Son? We're already late, you know. Shall we go back after it?" Timur slowed the car down, waiting for Miles to answer.

Now, it happened that I had been on an overnight visit to Timur's house so I was riding in the front seat the next morning when Timur drove Dylan and Miles to school. I heard the little exchange between Miles and Timur, and the long pause before Miles answered his father.

"No, Papa. Never mind, thank you. Let's go to school."

"All right, Son," Timur responded, and continued driving down the hill to the school. I had just turned my head to compliment Miles on his decision, when I heard him murmur as if to himself: "I was thinking it was time to leave it behind, anyway."

Everything had its own time and place in Miles' world, it seemed. I can still remember other incidents that illustrated this. When he was still a tiny toddler barely able to walk, Timur brought Miles and his older brother Dylan to visit me in my new apartment in Edmonds. They were full of excitement to see where *Baba Anne (father's mother, in Turkish)* was living now. Dylan, especially, had missed me; I'd been his morning playmate for over four years.

I invited them to look around in the different rooms, but to respect everything, and to leave Auntie Hikmet's room absolutely alone. She was setting up her computer and it was "complicated." When it was all set up, she promised to invite them in for a computer game.

So I told my little visitors there were new books on the Boys' Bookshelf. Dylan helped himself to a book and sat down to look at it. I started to offer a little book to Miles, but it was a bit dusty and I reached for a tissue to wipe off the dust. Then I crumpled up the tissue and tossed it into the wicker basket near the bookshelf.

I missed the basket, but ignored it, thinking I'd pick up the bit of paper when I got up from my easy chair. Dylan was too absorbed in his book to notice this, but little Miles noticed it. Then so did I.

I watched as Miles silently toddled over to the basket, picked up the tissue from the floor, dropped it in the basket, and toddled back to look at his book. The child was barely walking, and not even talking yet. His sense of orderliness made a lasting impression on me.

What is this neat child going to be when he grows up? I wondered. Probably a scientist, or an engineer working in an orderly world, where everything has a place, and everything fits in its place.

EPILOGUE   *I've noticed that rather than following in his brother's footsteps, observant Miles tries to figure out something when he doesn't understand it. Then, if he can't work it out himself, he asks Dylan or Papa to explain.*

Although there's nearly four years difference in age, Miles loves to play with Dylan; they are both encouraged by their parents to respect each other and be "best friends."

Dylan is a patient tutor to Miles: he explains the tricks in a game to him, and he demonstrates the wrestling moves he learned from their cousin Gordon, now a twelfth-grader.

For their birthdays, both boys got roller blades so they could skate in the closed-off driveway in front of their house. Soon, they graduated to skateboards, and drifted away from baseball. When they showed an interest in basketball, Papa Timur put up a family basketball hoop at the end of the garden, where he sometimes joins them shooting hoops after work.

Miles has always enthusiastically striven to keep up with his brother in sports. Strangely, however, he refused to enter the pool at the YMCA gym, or even to entertain the idea of swimming lessons. This was true, even though their mother Paige enrolled brother Dylan when he was about a year and a half old. By the age of three, Dylan was doing laps the length of the pool, and by the age of four or so was high-diving with advanced children.

Again, strangely, Miles decided all of a sudden one day to start swimming lessons, and it wasn't long after his orientation to the pool that he announced he "loved the water."

In addition to swimming, fishing, and camping with Papa, both boys have developed a keen interest in the international game of soccer. This goes back to their paternal grandfather Selahattin Malkoç, who had encouraged son Timur as a small child to kick a soccer ball with the other boys in our neighborhood. This was in the small petroleum-refinery town of Batman near the Tigris River in southeastern Turkey.

I never was a soccer fan, per se, only the mother of one. I remember clearly, however, that my son Timur barely knew ten words at the age of two, but whenever he kicked the soccer ball, one of those early words was "Goal!"   Now, my grandson Dylan plays Left Forward, and is considered an excellent soccer player in the sixth grade at the Mukilteo Middle School. He has what I would describe as a charismatic personality, drawing other children to him when he appears on the playground.

154

As for the more reserved little third-grader Miles, he plays Center Forward. According to his father, Miles is a focused player. "He seems to see the whole field."

Although lighter in build than many of the other players on his team, young Miles makes up for it in speed and strategy, darting in and out to pass or kick his goals.

"Miles changes the complexion of the game when he enters the field," his father claims. This year, Miles is the team captain, highly thought of by the other teams, according to Timur. The boys' parents take turns driving them to their various games, which this year includes la crosse, a new challenge for the two brothers.

Miles relaxing in blue jeans and favorite sweater

18

MY EXOTIC PEN PAL
An Interview *with a* 4th Grade Writing Class
Mukilteo, Washington 2006

PROLOGUE   At the time of this story, my ten-year-old grandson Dylan was in Mrs. Idso's writing class for fourth-graders in elementary school in Mukilteo, Washington.

Although she also taught science, it was to Mrs. Idso's writing class that I was invited; Dylan had told her his grandmother was a writer and had published some books. True, that year I had written a collection of short stories, and self-published it under the title: "Dreams & Other True Tales." So I sent Mrs. Idso a copy, with a note explaining I usually wrote only from personal experience, and never attempted fiction.

To celebrate the printing of "Dreams," my daughter Melike Eden had arranged a book reading in her neighborhood clubhouse in South Seattle. Afterward, she asked the circle of guests to introduce themselves, and tell how they had met the author.

At the end of the circle, my son Timur stood up to introduce himself as the author's son; his seven-year-old son Miles followed suit. Then eleven-year-old Dylan did likewise, adding: "My Baba Anne (father's mother, in Turkish) is a writer, and she writes books. I'm proud of her. I want to be a writer when I grow up." I was quite surprised, and felt terribly proud of Dylan.

The new topic in Mrs. Idso's fourth-grade writing class that month was "Writing and Publishing Books." When she invited me to visit Dylan's class, I told her I'd be delighted, and asked: "What should I prepare?"

"It's up to you," she said. "They will interview you about your writing, and how you got started publishing. I'm leaving the questions up to them. The class is one-hour long."

By the age of 82, I had already retired twice, and was settled comfortably into a quiet life of leisurely writing. So now, it took me some time to envision myself in a classroom of lively elementary-school children. I had to think carefully about this visit.

First of all, to introduce some basic tips about writing that I'd gleaned over the years, I composed a light-hearted verse in bookmark form. I laminated enough copies for the class, hoping to inspire the youthful writers. *See copy in Appendix.*

I also rummaged through my "Precious Old Papers" folder and found samples of writing from my childhood, and several books I had written and "self-published." That's enough preparation for the visit, I thought; the rest is in my head.

That morning I woke up early, dressed warmly, had a good breakfast, and was ready when Timur came to take me to Dylan's class in Mukilteo Elementary School.

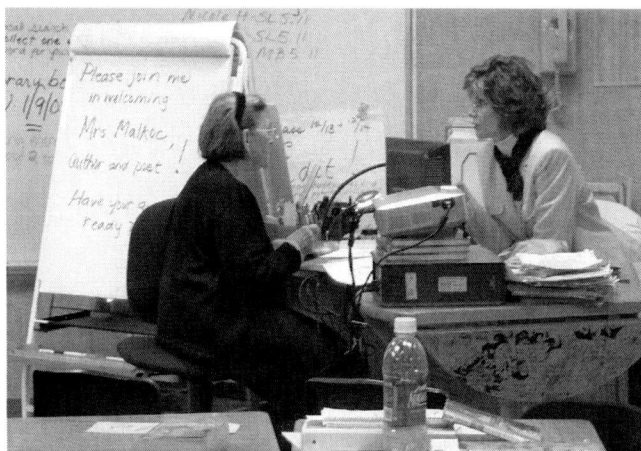

The writing teacher, Mrs. Idso, talking to the author (seated)

When Timur and I walked into Mrs. Idso's classroom, introductions were brief, and really unnecessary, thanks to Dylan. Wasting no time, I immediately handed out and read my introduction. *(See Appendix.)*

Now, it was Question Time for the students. One boy asked about my first writing experience. As soon as I'd learned to print with a pencil, I told him, my mother showed me how to send a message on a penny-postcard to my cousin who lived 70 miles away on a wheat farm. That summer, she and I sent penny-postcards to each other every week.

My mother had also told me I could write a short message on a card and mail it almost anywhere in the world. All I needed to do was spell the name correctly, and write the address correctly. Just imagine: in those days, one penny-postcard cost only a cent!

After all these years, I still remember how the idea of mailing penny-postcards to the far corners of the world seemed like magic to me. I showed the children several postcards I'd written when I was about their age, or younger. I've always kept them in my "Precious Old Papers" folder, I explained, because I've never had the heart to throw them away.

I asked the children in Mrs. Idso's writing class about Pen Pals; they all had Pen Pals, they responded — some in Mexico, or in Canada, some as far away as China.

The author asks about Pen Pals.

When I was about 13 years old, I told the class, Pen Pals was a brand-new idea. The Pen Pal Organization notified public schools in the United States how school children could get on the Pen Pal list: Just write a short letter with their name and address, and put a dime in the envelope. When their letters reached the general Pen Pal office, they would be matched up with the names of children in other states, or in other countries on other continents.

It sounded like a tremendously exciting idea to *me* — a penny-postcard writer! This was back in 1938, still the Great Depression years, I reminded the children. At that time, I knew that one dime — 10 cents —was the price of two whole loaves of bread, and two loaves of bread made a lot of sandwiches for our growing family. My mother had to count every penny carefully "to make the money stretch."

How would *I* ever get a dime to buy a name on the Pen Pal list? I had never *owned* a dime. So, the idea of joining Pen Pals seemed as far away as a fairy tale.

Nevertheless, I was obliged to take the Pen Pals announcement home to my mother. Nervously, I gave her the paper and waited while she read it. I remember how slowly she reached down into the bottom of her mysterious apron pocket, and how slowly she pulled out a little silver dime. "Here," she said. "Take this, and write a letter!"

On afterthought, she left the room quickly, rummaged through her desk, and returned with a three-cent postage stamp. "Here," she said, "Take this for the envelope!"

I was too amazed at this unexpected generosity to say anything but "Thank you, Mama." I took the dime and the stamp to my teacher the next day. I remember following her instructions carefully. First, I washed my hands carefully in the schoolroom washbasin, sharpened my pencil in the pencil sharpener, and helped myself to a clean sheet of ruled paper from the supply table. Then, with the utmost care, I wrote my first *real* letter. It wasn't long, but limited to short statements about my hometown near the Spokane River, and the fact that I had one sister and five brothers. Also, I enjoyed geography, writing postcards, and bus travel. I omitted the fact that we were very poor during the Depression; that was not *un*usual. Most people I knew were poor in those days.

I took great pains to write within the margins of the paper and to make no spelling mistakes, so the teacher passed inspection on my writing. She handed me an envelope, showed me step-by-step how to write the address on it, fold my letter properly with the dime inside, slip it inside the envelope, then stick the stamp on the upper right-hand corner. When I sealed up the envelope, it was ready to mail.

I could hardly wait for school to let out that afternoon so I could hurry to the corner mailbox and drop my letter down the slot. As it slid down out of view, I felt a flash of excitement. *I had mailed a letter to a Pen Pal!*

A lot of time must have passed after mailing my letter, I told my young listeners, but I was unaware of it. School life was so exciting and full of daily challenges in those days that all thoughts of pen pal letters quickly passed out of my head.

In fact, some three months passed. One afternoon as I walked home from school, I was surprised to see my mother waiting for me on the sidewalk in front of our house. This was unusual for her. I also noticed that she was holding a blue envelope in her hand.

"The mailman brought this letter for you today," she said, handing it to me with a little smile. It was the first time I'd ever received a *letter* in the mail, with my name on the envelope! I opened it on the spot.

As I finished the first part of this story of my Pen Pal letter, I made a small bow to the class, and pulled out a blue envelope from my

"Precious Old Papers" folder. "Can you guess what this is?" I asked the children.

"Your pen pal letter!" they shouted.

"Right!" I responded. "Now, guess where it's from!" I carefully extracted the letter from it and passed the blue envelope around the room. No one recognized the stamp or the postmark.

"Now, I'm going to read a paragraph from my pen pal's letter. Listen carefully, because when I read one sentence, I nearly *fainted!*"

I took a deep breath as I unfolded the blue letter-paper, and looked once again at the once beautiful handwriting that had been so crisp on the page. I thought to myself: *So many years have passed since the first time I read this letter. . .   Am I releasing a genie out of an antique bottle now? Or, will I swoon as I nearly did at the first reading, right there on the sidewalk on Third Avenue in Spokane, Washington?* I took another deep breath, and began to read bits from the letter written by my pen pal more than 70 years earlier:

"Dear Miss Jones,"

"Thank you for your letter. Now I will introduce myself. I am a schoolboy, fifteen years of age. I am in good health, sturdy, of dark (but not black) complexion. I have a brother and sister, a father and mother . . ."

Here, I paused and looked up at the children for questions. No one had a clue about the origin of the writer.

I went on to read another sentence: *"I live in Poona, and my father is the Rajah of Poona…"*

I stopped the letter again. "As I told you, when I first read this last sentence, over 70 years ago," I said to the mystified children, "I nearly fainted!"

"Why?" asked a boy in the back row.

"Well, do you know what a *rajah* is?" I asked him.

He didn't know. Then I asked the class in general. No one had a clue. So, I had to answer my own question:

"*I* knew what a rajah was, because my mother took me to the new Carnegie Library, and I read all the *"Fairy Tales from around the World"* that summer. There were pictures of rajahs riding down the street in — guess what country? Where is Poona?"

I stopped again, put the world globe on a front desk and waited for someone to volunteer an answer. Timidly, the children ventured guesses: "China? Africa?" "Afghanistan?" Finally, "India?"

"Right! *India!*" I smiled at the good guesser, and signaled someone in the front row to twirl the globe to India, and hold it up for the class to see.

"Now, when a rajah came to visit," I continued to explain, "he would send a man to carry a picture in advance, so the people would know who was arriving. Then people would sprinkle fresh flowers along the street, and musicians would play sweet music. Finally, the rajah himself would arrive, riding on a —— Guess what?" Again I paused.

"Horse? Jeep? Donkey? Bicycle? Camel? Airplane?" The class exhausted their imagination.

"None of the above! He would come riding on an *elephant!* Imagine that! Rajahs rode on huge elephants, with golden decorations, sitting in a fancy *howdah* — or seat — on top of the elephant," I waved and gestured upward. "Wa-a-ay up there! Of course, a special servant would bring a ladder so the rajah could climb up there gracefully."

"Just imagine!" I laughed at the thought. "My pen pal's father was a rich rajah — a Hindu ruler in India! On the other hand, my own father was *not* rich; he was a mechanic in Spokane, Washington. *(My Papa never used the word "poor." He always referred to himself as "hardworking.")*

Furthermore, my Papa never rode elephants. He walked to work — or sometimes drove his old Ford truck!" I laughed again at the contrasts. "Imagine that! My pen pal's papa was a *rajah!*"

A serious girl in the third row asked: "Did you answer the letter? And what did you write about?"

I nodded. "Yes, I answered the letter. I wrote about my favorite books, and what we were studying in geography."

"Did your Pen Pal ever write again?" came the next question.

"I don't really know," I answered her, picking up the blue envelope and pointing out where it was marked ***PASSED by CENSOR*** on one end of the envelope. This was in 1940, as I recall, but the postmark date wasn't very clear.

"This was just before the beginning of the Second World War in Europe," I explained to the class. "At the same time, there was unrest in India, an ancient country, where the people wanted to be independent from Great Britain so the Indian government checked all the letters coming into, and going out of the country. If someone wrote bad things or dangerous things about the government in India, the post office had to censor (black) it out, with black ink."

"And then, there were revolutionary wars in India," I continued sadly. "I think a better answer to your question may be that I never *received* another letter from my pen pal. He may have written one, perhaps, and it was censored and never sent to me. Or perhaps my pen pal's family moved away."

The children had a number of other questions to ask, including an especially good one: "What inspired you most to write, Mrs. Malkoç?"

At this question, many events, books, and people who had inspired me over the years rushed through my head. I had a vivid flashback of writing my first newspaper article, when I was living in Turkey around 1960. By that time, I was married, and had several small children, I told the class. My mother knew a newspaper editor in my hometown of Spokane, Washington, and when she mentioned to the editor that she had a married daughter living in Turkey, he said it would be "interesting" to hear about life in that part of the world.

He sent me a letter asking if I would write an article about Turkey for his Sunday paper. Because I'd never written a newspaper article before, the idea really made me nervous. What subject should I choose? Obviously, it should be something I knew well, something from my own experience, and, especially, something of interest to American readers. It took me several days to come up with a good topic for an article: *Four Weddings in Turkey*. I decided I would describe some very different marriage celebrations I'd attended during my years in Turkey. *(See reference to "Four Weddings in Turkey" in Appendix Notes.)*

So, for several weeks, I scribbled down my thoughts in dozens of notes, wrote down short paragraphs, organized my information into four rough outlines (one for each event), then wrote a long paragraph for each section, and finally wrote out a draft of the whole article.

I read and reread the paragraphs to polish them up. This took me another week. Then I spent many days *typing* it all out carefully on my old portable typewriter — without making any mistakes! (If I made a mistake, I had no way of correcting it. I would have to retype the whole page.)

Finally, I put all the typewritten pages in a strong envelope, and addressed it to the Editor of the *Spokesman-Review* newspaper in Spokane, Washington, USA. I mailed it from the little post office in the tiny oil refinery town of Batman, located near the Tigris River in the southeastern corner of Turkey.

Several months after sending my article to the Spokane editor, I received a large manila envelope in the mail. "Can anyone guess what it was?" I asked the class. "No? Well, it was my article about four Turkish weddings — a full-page spread in the Sunday newspaper, in the *Culture and Arts* section! The reason I remember this so clearly, 50 years later, I explained to the class, was this: When I read that large newspaper page carefully, I realized what the editor had done. Rather, what he had *not* done. *He had not changed anything in my article! He had not changed or left out one part! He had printed every word!*

Now, what do you think that meant to me?"

There was silence in the classroom until one small voice timidly piped up: "He thought it was OK?"

"You're *right!*" I nodded and smiled at the good guesser. "The editor must have liked my writing! Otherwise, he wouldn't have put it in his newspaper, would he? I was so *encouraged!* I was *inspired* to try to write professionally!"

At this point, although there were other students with questions, I could see Mrs. Idso pointing to the schoolroom clock. It was her silent signal that my hour was up, so I thanked her and her students for the visit. I wished them all the best of luck with their own writing in the future. And I told them how inspiring their questions were for *me!*

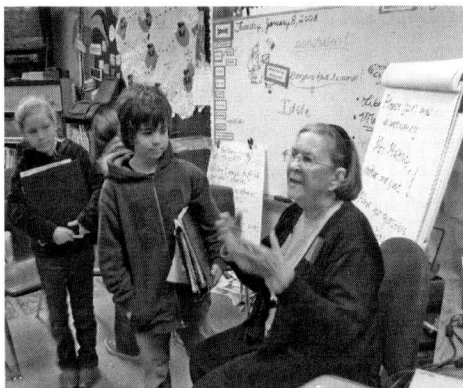

The author answers questions while Dylan waits his turn.

Timur, who had brought me to the classroom and had been taking pictures on his camcorder, was waiting to take me home. "Thank you for taking me to school today, Son. I had a wonderful visit!" I told him. "Now, I think I'll just go in and rest my eyes."

165

No sooner had I stretched out in my easy chair and closed my eyes, than I fell into a deep sleep. Apparently, during that one hour in the classroom, I had completely used up all my energy, for I slept for three hours, like a log!

EPILOGUE I. *To celebrate finishing a previous collection of short stories, I flew off for a six-week visit to relatives and friends in Turkey.*

As usual, I collected postcards to send home to my grandsons in Mukilteo. One picture from the famous Topkapi Museum in Istanbul especially caught my eye: a photograph of an Indian elephant, approximately the size of an American football, made of 22-carat gold. The gold elephant stood atop an oblong music box also made of gold. Its only decoration was a wide gold band studded with a row of chunky jewels: lustrous pearls, sparkling rubies, diamonds, sapphires, and emeralds all as large as robins' eggs.

*The caption under the music box read: **"Gift to the Sultan of Turkey, from India."** I couldn't resist sending that postcard to Dylan with a whimsical message: "Do you think this gift could have been from my pen pal's papa, the Rajah of Poona?"*

As I dropped the postcard in the mailbox, I thought to myself: "Stranger things have happened in life!"

EPILOGUE II. *My eldest daughter, Hikmet, who had been scanning all the photographs and graphics for this collection of short stories, was happy to read the addition to Dylan's writing class interview.*

"Just imagine, Mother," she said, "two young schoolchildren living on the other side of the world from each other — one in India and one in America — both writing in the same language! Hmmm. I wonder what ever happened to your Pen Pal?"

She did a quick bit of mental arithmetic and continued: "He was your age, wasn't he? Born in 1925. So he'd be eighty four years old this year."

Then, picking up my folder with the decades-old letter from my Pen Pal (the letter that had cost a precious dime and a three-cent stamp in those Depression days), she checked the name and address printed carefully on its envelope. As she left the room, I heard her murmur, "I think I'll look him up on the Internet."

I thought of the historic world changes and global wars that had taken place since that little letter was postmarked in the 1940s in Poona, India. I was about to say: "That was long ago and a lifetime away, Hikmet Dear. Don't waste your time looking for something that is long gone!" But I held my tongue.

Instead, I went out for my afternoon walk in the lovely spring weather, where the radiant sun was shining on the beautiful snowcapped peaks, and on the sailboats out on Puget Sound, as they made their way inland from the Pacific Ocean.

When I returned from my walk that afternoon, daughter Hikmet showed me all the information she'd found on the Internet concerning my Pen Pal and his family — including color photographs of the palace his father (the previous Rajah) had turned into a boys and girls school, and the new school my Pen Pal had built for poor girls in his hometown when he became the Rajah.

As I understand it, before the Rajah of Poona and his son passed away, they both had established a number of schools to help educate poor children in their province.

Other information that my daughter Hikmet found on the Internet included some photographs with Bombay's new name: Mumbai, Maharashtra.

She printed out two long pages of descendents of the first Rajah of the dynasty of Naik Nimbalkar, founded in 1270 in the princely state of Phaltan. May they all rest in peace.

EPILOGUE III. *Several years after that wonderfully exhilarating visit to grandson Dylan's 4th-grade writing class, and after my last visit to Turkey, I had an informal telephone interview with Dylan. I wanted to hear about his recent summer cruise with his maternal grandmother Jacquie; they had sailed roundtrip on the "Sapphire Princess" (capacity 3,000 passengers) from Seattle to Alaska and back.*

These popular cruise ships stop at various little seaports along the way, so passengers may debark and walk about, shop for Native American handicrafts, and take photos of the picturesque towns and magnificent seascapes. One of the scheduled stops for the "Sapphire Princess" was the small town of Skagway in Southeast Alaska, near the historical Klondike gold fields.

Observant twelve-year-old Dylan, who has always been fascinated by interesting art and clothing — especially headgear — noticed a group of several dozen people, some wearing "familiar looking headscarves," he told me. (There are lots of photos of grandmothers, aunts, and girl cousins wearing headscarves in his Papa's photograph albums.)

He walked close enough to hear them speaking some language that was not English, so he walked even closer. Then he recognized the language they were speaking was Turkish.

According to what Dylan told his Auntie Hikmet, he simply walked right up to the group, and to their amazement, addressed them in Turkish: "Merhaba!" (Hello.) And then a few other polite phrases he had learned from his Papa, from me (his Baba Anne), and from his aunties Hikmet and Kâmuran.

I imagine that Dylan quite soon ran out of basic vocabulary, but he was able to understand that the Turkish-speaking tourists were curious about where he and his family came from. "Were they interesting? What did you learn from them, Dylan?" I asked him. He had to think quite a while to answer.

I tried another tack: "Well, Dylan, would you say they were friendly?"

He thought for another moment, and nodded. "Yes, they were friendly."

"How could you tell, Dylan?"

"Their eyes twinkled. And they smiled a lot," he answered.

APPENDIX: STORY NOTES

Note for TALE 2: Life on a Wheat Farm

Note 1: My Cousin Lucile's Half-Brother Merle

When I first visited my Cousin Lucile, I was perhaps three. It was hard to learn the names and attach them to the relatives when we didn't visit them often, and it was some years before I ever saw her half-brother Merle. I was in grade school the summer I finally got to see him. He happened to be at the farm when my parents went to visit and took me along to play with Lucile.

Later that day, after he'd left with his father and uncles to return to Spokane, Lucile explained who Merle was: Uncle Elsworth's son by his first wife, who had died a "long time ago." Merle was "frail," she added, and needed "special care," so he stayed in Spokane, to be near a hospital. I understood that it was something about his liver.

My dim recollection of Merle's face is that he was nice looking, with dark hair, combed neatly, and wore glasses. He seemed to be about my oldest brother David's age, but he didn't run or sprint, like David did, or tinker with radios, either. He mostly read books, or took a nap, or just rested in bed.

I remember Merle more clearly when he was brought to the farm for his last visit (as it turned out). I may have been about 11 or 12 then.

His room was full of relatives, mainly his aunts and uncles and boy cousins, each taking a turn talking to him as he lay in his bed. He would ask a question quietly about a favorite cow, for example: "What did you name the new calf?" Or about the farm: "How many bushels an acre, this year, Cousin Bill?" He seemed to be keeping up with the farm, all right. And keeping up with other relatives: "How is Aunt Hannah Jane?" he asked another aunt. "Did she win a blue ribbon for her angel food cake this year?"

He was talking quietly, so everyone else in the room was talking quietly. One by one, people took their turn to tell a bit of family news, tell a new joke, give Merle a pat on the shoulder and a smile as they waved goodbye and left the room (before they "wore him out," Aunt Ann said.)

Eventually, there was no one else in the room but just Cousin Lucile and me. She motioned that it was my turn. "I don't have anything to report to him. What shall I do?" I whispered to her.

"Just say hello," she whispered.

I nodded, and moved toward the bed. Merle already had his hand out. It was cold when I started to shake it, so I just leaned over and whispered, "I'm Anna Marie."

"*I know,*" he whispered back. I ventured a small smile and he smiled back a little. At this point, I could see Aunt Ann signaling it was time to leave, and Cousin Lucile rescued me.

"We'll see you next visit, Merle," Lucile said in her sweet voice. "Bye for now!"

"*Next visit,*" I whispered to Merle. I smiled a little more, and waved to him as I sidled out the door.

I think Merle died not long after that visit, and the funeral was held in Uncle Elsworth's church in Wilbur. We couldn't go for some reason; probably Papa had a repair job and needed the money, since it was still in the Depression Days.

I think of Cousin Lucile often. Now and then, I think about how lucky I was, to grow up with a sister and five brothers, while Lucile had only a half-brother, part of her life. It made me feel too lucky in a way; I didn't do anything to deserve it, and it didn't seem fair to her at all.

Notes for TALE 3: *The* HOUSE *at* "ROCKY ACRES"

Note 1. Indian Canyon and Local Roads
The wooded canyon, west of Spokane Falls at the bend of Government Way, was called Indian Canyon after its earliest known inhabitants. (*See following Note 2 on the Spokane Tribe.*)

The road on the plateau rimming the canyon above, from the old Sunset Highway — now Highway 2 — to the Palisades basalt rock formation on the Rim, was known as Rimrock Drive. The road above, closely paralleling the Rimrock, is now officially listed as Basalt Drive, but at the time of my family's story, the official Spokane County Courthouse surveyors' plats referred to the narrow dirt road that ran through our property as Rural Route 4.

Note 2: The local Spokane Tribe The following excerpts are adapted from the *Wellpinit School District March 15, 2009*, published by the Spokane Indian Reservation, and accessed from the Internet, Wikipedia: According to historians, the Spokane tribe of Native Americans had settled in "permanent winter villages" where fish were plentiful, perhaps in the 13th century.

"... There were three bands or groups of Spokanes living in the wooded regions around the Spokane River, with the Spokane Falls their center of trade and fishing... Sharing their language and territory were the Colville, Flathead, and Kalispel tribes.

The Spokanes were hunters and gatherers. The regional forests and fields provided them with plentiful deer and bear, also smaller animals including beaver, muskrat, porcupines, martens and coyotes. They also hunted partridge, pheasant, and smaller fowl of the region.

During the spring salmon runs in the Spokane River, they speared great numbers of fish — which they smoked and ate throughout the cold winter months, when hunting was difficult or impossible... In addition, they dug up many varieties of edible roots and plants, including balsam and camas roots, wild carrots and onions, and cattails. From the plentiful bushes, they gathered hazelnuts, chokecherries, hawthorn berries, service berries and other wild fruit..."
[End of excerpt]

The majority of the Spokane tribal members long ago moved from the Spokane River and Indian Canyon areas to settle on reservations. Many married outside their tribe and mingled into the local communities. Others moved to work or attend schools and universities in other localities. Myriad remnants from their existence in these parts are preserved in local museums, where they are treasured and kept for future generations.

Years after John's memorable scouting expedition on Route 4, some of his sharp-eyed children and grandchildren discovered perfect arrow heads along the Rimrock. They have also turned up many bits and pieces of agate arrowheads in the basalt rock quarry. John thinks because the tips were defective, the arrowhead makers simply tossed them into their campfires.

Historians tell us that the Spokane River and Indian Canyon areas once were plentiful sources of food, and the woods teemed with wildlife. In the spring, the river ran thick with spawning salmon. "So thick a man could walk across the fish," reported one anonymous fisherman of the time. Sadly, the bountiful fish have decreased in number, and the wildlife as well, so Indian Canyon has been designated as a preservation area. Hunting there has been outlawed for many years.

Note 3. Basalt Rock
The dictionary defines basalt as the hard black volcanic rock produced by the partial melting of the Earth's mantle (the part of the Earth lying

between the crust and the core of the Earth). Basalt covers more than half of the Earth's surface.

Note 4. The Old Stone Quarry

My brother John always enjoyed talking with the "Old Timers" in the Rimrock and Garden Springs neighborhood. From them, he learned a lot about the history of the area.

At the turn of the 19th century, John was told, the pothole up on the hill had indeed been a working stone quarry. Master stonemasons were employed to cut the basalt rock for the foundations of some South Hill homes. Some of the cobblestones commissioned by the City of Spokane to line streetcar tracks on the South Hill also came from the old quarry on the "Rocky Acres" hill.

Note 5. Who Else Had Lived on This Property before Us? The Chinese Gardener and the Japanese Gardeners

It was some years later that John heard about the Chinese gardener who had lived on the property many years before our family arrived on the scene. John does not believe he was the person who dug the cased well under the trees by the road. Rather, John guesses, his source of water was probably one of the many springs that were said to have existed in the marshlands around there at that time.

The anonymous Chinese gardener had arrived from China probably sometime in the mid or late 1800's, at a time when the immigration laws allowed Chinese laborers to enter the U.S.

He had managed somehow to acquire the small piece of meadowland along Route 4, where, according to hearsay, he raised lettuce, squash, radishes, cucumbers, green onions, and other fresh vegetables to sell in the Farmers' Market in downtown Spokane.

Because the soil was watered by underground springs in the area above Indian Canyon, the Chinese gardener's vegetables flourished; it was said that he could grow multiple crops during one season. His days began before dawn, we may assume, rising to pick the bountiful produce, then driving it by horse cart into town to sell it in the market. His circumstances would have forced him to live frugally, saving every penny he could until he had enough to send for his wife, waiting back home in China.

Unfortunately, by the time he had earned enough to send for her, even more restrictive "Exclusionary" immigration laws had been enacted. These laws barred wives of Chinese laborers from entering the U.S. to join their husbands already living here. *[These restrictive laws, however, did not apply to Chinese merchants and diplomats, who were free to enter the U.S.]*

Sadly, the transplanted Chinese gardener was forced to return to the land of his birth, leaving nothing behind to mark his long years of lonely toil in the meadow above the Rimrock. Again according to hearsay, the small piece of land the gardener from China had relinquished on Route 4 was eventually acquired by Japanese gardeners, who carried on their truck gardening in the meadow along the road for some time — long enough to put up a small shack and drill a 74-foot cased well under the tall pine trees facing the road.

In time, however, the Japanese gardeners resettled in the nearby Garden Springs area, where other Japanese families were already well established with their gardens.

Note 6. The Neighborhood "Little Red One-Room School House" and the Japanese School Friends

When the rural school zoning was changed in the 1940's, my younger brothers Pete and Mike were officially required to transfer from the Occident School (known as "The Little Red One-Room Schoolhouse" located west of Route 4), to the consolidated Garden Springs school across Sunset Highway. My brothers remained life-long friends with their Japanese classmates in Garden Springs. My brother Mike has been teaching English in Japan for over 40 years; his wife Miyako is also an English teacher.

Note 7. Cousin Donald

Donald Francis Roy, the only child of Mama's sister Suzanne Harms Roy, was newly married to Virginia Kinnebrew from California at the time he had volunteered to help Papa on our house. He was planning to build a little house of his own down the road. He knew next to nothing about carpentry, but he was a fast learner, and this was an ideal learning opportunity for him.

Cousin Donald's established professional field was sociology. He had already graduated from the U. of Washington with Phi Beta Kappa honors, later went on to earn a PhD. at the U. of Chicago, and eventually became a tenured professor at Duke University.

Note 8. Naming the Place "Rocky Acres"

Mama named our new home on Route 4 right after she chose a spot for her vegetable garden and started to dig around.

"Try digging anywhere around here, you only run into rock!" she exclaimed. Mama, it should be mentioned, had lady friends who named their summer homes fancifully: "The Willows," "Bide-a-Wee," "Fisherman's Rest," and "Emerald Acres," but Mama wanted a name that was unpretentious and fitting.

"Rocky Acres!" she announced prophetically as she struck another rock sharply with her spade, and went on with her digging. The name stuck.

Actually, Mama was a *born* name-giver. She gave names to all the animals she ever had. Napoleon and Josephine, for instance, were her pet bantam chickens cooped in our backyard on Third Avenue. Tiny Napoleon was naturally given to strutting his feathers and crowing, while tiny Josephine was merely beautiful, and quietly domestic. During Josephine's laying season, Mama trained her to follow the stale bread crumb trail every morning all the way up to our back porch, scratch on the screen door to come in, then hop up and lay an egg in her basket atop the kitchen stove's wood-box. She would then cluck, hop down and retrace her path out of the kitchen, to more crumbs waiting for her on the porch.

Romantically named Chloe was the next animal Mama acquired after we moved to Route 4 — an old white goat that lived in a pen across the road and a little way up the hill. She was given to bleating mournfully at odd hours of the night, and her name was inspired by an old blues ballad: *Chloe, in the dark of night, I hear you calling my name, Chlo-o-o-eee!*

Chloe was quietly swapped one day to make way for Modie, the "new French goat." Mama pointed out that Modie was a real improvement over Chloe: Modie was a talented lawn trimmer, especially the hard-to-reach edges of the lawn around the house.

For weeks, we all tried to guess the origin of Modie's name, but to no avail. Mama finally broke down one day and confessed the French goat's name *Modie* was simply short for *Mow de Lawn.*

Our next family pet, Sugar-the-Blind-Horse, was the exact color of brown sugar. Although past his prime, the gentle creature was well fed and cared for, and the little children loved to ride him.

His other rather unmentionable but still valuable asset was that he was a patient provider of fertilizer for the garden.

Note 9. Installing Heating Ducts in the Sawdust Furnace

For some time, Papa had been considering heating systems for the house, and finally arrived at a simple but ingenious system that could operate on a free source of fuel: sawdust. He consulted with acquaintances who had the kind of information he needed, made detailed floor plans and measurements for each room to be heated, then ordered sheet metal to be cut for the flues that would carry the heated air from the sawdust-burning furnace in the basement up to the ground floor and upstairs rooms.

After the heating ducts were installed under the floors, they required a careful and special examination. Little six-year-old Mike was chosen for this job, as he was bright enough to follow orders, and still small enough to crawl through the sheet-metal ducts.

On the day of the examination, he listened attentively to Papa's instructions: "Start at one end and crawl your way through to the other end, checking for obstructions. Remember, I'll be following every inch of your progress from the other side." When Mike reached the end of the ductwork, he shouted out as instructed: "The coast is clear!" before crawling out. Papa took Mike outside, thoroughly dusted him off, and praised him effusively.

Then, with a ceremonious flick of his wrist, he turned on the new furnace, and like magic — and unlike our first (basalt) fireplace — everything worked faultlessly. The electric furnace-fan wafted the heated air upward through the heating ducts and into each room on the first and second floors of the little house.

More than fifteen years passed before Anna Maria retired and bought the house from brothers Pete and Mike. She had a strict renovation of the house done, including the plumbing and electrical wiring systems. At that time, all the asbestos fireproofing (the only kind of insulation in use at the time of installation) was carefully removed and disposed of according to strict new government regulations banning its use.

Note for TALE 6: *RICH WHITMAN'S DAY SCHOOL*
The author's *Easy Plays in English* was first published by Metro Books in Istanbul, and then by Warsaw Pedagogical State Textbook Publishing in Warsaw. After the author retired, Prentice-Hall/Pearson Publishing in New Jersey, USA published the third (revised) edition.

Note for TALE 15: *GORDON AT THE DOLL FESTIVAL*
During the 1920s, relations between America and Japan were strained when the Immigration Act of 1924 prohibited East Asians from immigrating to the US. Many people encouraged goodwill between the two countries, including Dr. Sidney Gulick, author, educator, and missionary, who had loved Japan and lived there for 25 years.

Dr. Gulick was a visionary. He initiated a program in which American schoolchildren saved their pennies to send 'Blue-Eyed

Friendship Dolls' to schoolchildren in Japan. Each Friendship Doll was dressed in a traveling outfit, and had a wardrobe trunk, a favorite toy, a pocketbook holding her photograph, her passport with name and address, hankie, and other traveling necessities.

Nearly 13,000 Friendship Dolls were collected and packaged for travel on a steamship that carried them to Japan. Their voyage in 1927 was scheduled carefully so that they arrived at their destinations on *Hina Matsuri* (Doll Festival Day). They were received with great joy and celebration; a Japanese song, *The Blue-Eyed Dolls,* became wildly popular at that time.

In reciprocity, Japanese officials organized a program to send 58 Friendship Dolls from Japan, one for each of the 50 state capitals and the 8 territories. Each doll, made by a master doll maker to represent a province of Japan, was dressed in a beautiful silk kimono typical of that region. Each was a work of art.

Years passed, and world politics changed with the beginning of World War II. When Japan entered the war in 1941, some of the dolls were damaged or destroyed in anger, as they represented "the Face of the Enemy." Despite the tragic events of the war, many families and schoolteachers continued to love their Friendship Dolls and what they stood for; they hid their dolls in safe places. After the War, when peace finally came, people dug up their Friendship Dolls, one by one, from their hiding places all over Japan. Sadly, some had been totally destroyed, or lost. Happily, of the 58 original Japanese dolls sent to the U.S., nearly 50 have been located and restored. Most are in local museums or other public places on exhibit.

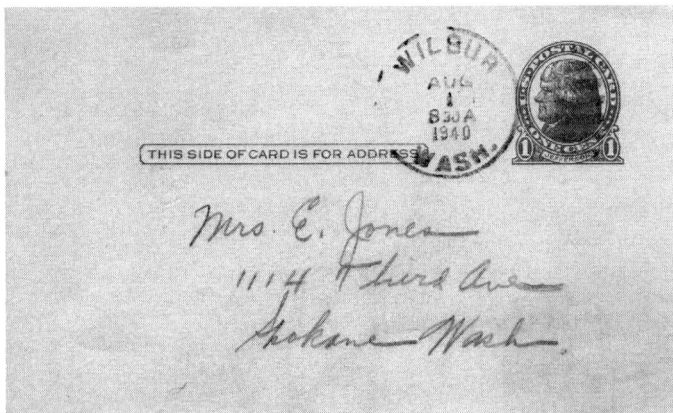

Penny post card to mother in Spokane WA,
From Wilbur WA, August 1, 1940

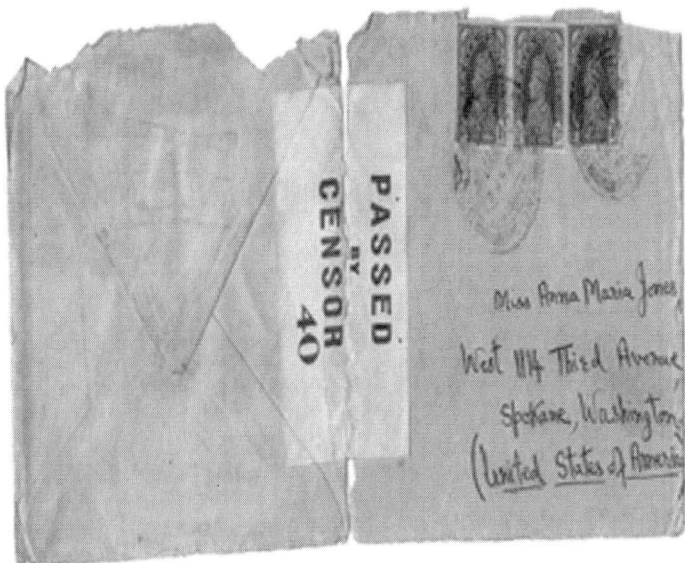

Envelope from Pen Pal in India,
Passed by CENSOR (c July 1939)

177

Manick Villa,
Deccan Gymkhana,
Poonah (India)
3rd January 40.

Dear miss Jones,

I was surprised to receive a letter from America,—that beautiful country of yours, of which I have read a lot in books and also seen a lot, but only in pictures. Yours happens to be the first letter that I have received from your distant land. I hope it won't prove to be the last and will surely be followed by many more.

I liked your letter so much. My reply to it will, I am afraid, be a tame affair. Yet I hope to make it interesting reading. I am a boy of fourteen. My hair is dark; so is my complexion, I can't call it black though. I am a very robust boy and weigh 135 lbs.

I go to the N.M.V. High-School which is the biggest school in Western India — over 2200 boys grouped into 55 divisions. Poona has a population of about 250000. It is not an industrial town, but it is an educational centre with as many as 10 colleges about 40 high-schools, and over 100 primary schools.

Ours is a day school. It has a very

Page One of my Pen Pal's Letter

extensive play grounds with arrangements for many Western and Indian games. I play cricket, football; badminton and do a lot of riding too.

Our school begins at 11·30 a.m. and is over by 4·30 p.m. I am a student of the sixth standard, and will enter the matriculation class next year. I learn Marathi (my mother-tongue), English, Arithmetic, Algebra, Geometry, History, Geography, Physics and Sanskrit. I like English, Maths though I don't dislike the other subjects. I am privately coached by three tutors.

I have got my parents, and three brothers and one sister. We are living in Poona for our education. My native place is Phaltan — a small state about 60 miles from Poona. My father is the Raja (or Ruler) of the state.

India is a tropical country, and we have no such thing as winter over this side of India, and the summer is very hot.

We have two long vacations during the year — the summer vacation (six weeks), and Diwali vacation (three weeks). Besides we get the X'mas holidays. I go on tours during the vacations. In the last vacation I had been in South-India and we may go to Delhi and Agra in the X'mas holidays.

PageTwo of my Pen Pal's Letter

I am sorry. I have not got a photograph of
my place on hand. I may send you one in my next. May I
expect some pictures from you about your place, your school--etc--
I believe I have troubled you with a lot of
informations. May I expect to hear more from you?

I remain,
Yours truly,
Vijaysinh M. Nimbalear.

Page Three of my Pen Pal's Letter

"To Very Young Writers"

How do you arrange words to express your thoughts?
Here are some suggestions, and some *caveats*:

Write what you *know* about. If not, leave it out!
Use the class dictionary, or encyclopedia in the library
to check out your facts; if unsure, give them the axe!
Then, *rewrite!*

If you're writing in your private diary, that's fine;
but if others are to read what is on your mind,
write and rewrite until it's clear and well defined.

Pianists, for example, practice difficult chords
over and over on their keyboards,
improving their skills through self-correction
until they reach a kind of perfection.

By careful rewriting and peer-correction,
writers also reach a kind of perfection.

Good writing skills will take you far,
no matter what you end up doing in life.
You may write to your boss, or a celebrity star,
Or, someday, to your husband or wife!
Or to Microsoft's billionaire, Bill Gates!
Or even to the President of the United States!

So, persevere, I say, in your writing each day;
and Good Luck to you in every way!

Mrs. Anna Maria Malkoç
Edmonds, Washington

SPECIAL PHOTOGRAPHS

Marie & Ethelbert Jones family photo, Spokane, Washington 1977

BACK ROW STANDING ON LEFT
1. **Uncle Harris Harms** *brother of Marie Harms Jones*
2. **Aunt Tret Harms** *wife of Harris Harms*
3. **Wallace (Wally) Phillipson** *husband of Camilla Jones Phillipson*
4. **John Harms Jones** *husband of Joyce McBride Jones*

BACK ROW SEATED:
5. **Joyce McBride Jones** *wife of John Harms Jones*
6. **Anna Maria Jones Malkoç** *(widow of Selahattin Malkoç)*
7. **Nona Pashek Jones** *wife of Aaron J. Jones*

BACK ROW STANDING ON RIGHT:
8. **Rosemary Nason Jones** *wife of David NMI Jones*
9. **Pete (Simeon Peter) Jones**

FRONT ROW KNEELING:
10. **Aaron J. Jones** *husband of Nona Pashek Jones*
11. **David NMI Jones** *husband of Rosemary Jones*
12. **Camilla Jones Phillipson** *wife of Wallace Phillipson*

Holiday photo, Washington DC, 1966
Anna Maria Malkoç with Kamuran & Hikmet (back row)
Melike & Timur (front row)

Gordon the Life-Guard, with cousins Dylan & Miles Malkoç
at a beach on Lake Washington, Seattle c 2007

Cousin Cihangir Malkoç, with Miles and Dylan Malkoç
Holidays 2009

Grandmother, Miles & Dylan Malkoç
Waiting at the AMTRAK station

ABOUT *the* AUTHOR

I was born in Spokane, Washington in 1925. Not surprisingly, in college I fell in love with an engineering student from the Black Sea, the first Turk I ever met. My whole family liked him at first sight, especially my mother: he chatted with her in German (her first language), and helped her weed her tomatoes. After receiving his MA, and his father's blessing, Sela and I married and spent most of the next ten years in the oilfields in Turkey. He was transferred to Ankara in 1962, and tragically, died in an auto accident in 1963.

Several years later, my children and I moved to the States. They adapted well, I worked at the Center for Applied Linguistics in DC, and earned an MA in linguistics. This led to a teaching grant in Poland, then to Foreign Service duties in Washington DC; Turkey; and Poland/Eastern Europe.

Retired at age 65, I spent the next decade teaching English/American studies at a beautiful Japanese Women's College in my hometown. Now, I'm a happily reflective, octogenarian autobiographer enjoying Grandmotherhood.   ***The Author***

AUTHOR'S BIBLIOGRAPHY

Books by the author available from: .
Bookstand Publishing: http://www.ebookstand.com
*Also, search under **MALKOC**.*

Tales from Rocky Acres: The Wildlife in My Garden
ISBN 1-58909-163-9
Easy-to-read true stories written for intermediate-level ESL students of English. These true stories will give you "food for thought." They are written in easy English, with easy language activities to stimulate conversation about these animals, birds, insects, and other creatures. Teacher's Edition also available.

A Bed of Roses: An American Woman's Memoirs from Turkey   ISBN 978-1-58909-286-0
As we were leaving New York Harbor in 1952, I asked my husband what life was really like in Turkey, and he answered thoughtfully; "Where we're going, I think life will not be a bed of roses!" While compiling these notes and dog-eared letters written some 60 years ago from oil fields in Turkey, my son asked what kind of book I was working on next. "A biography, with all the elements of a soap opera," I tell him. "Romance and adventure, danger and suspense, comedy and tragedy, divine inspiration, and in a way, a happy ending." Epistles, letters and postcard correspondence with family and friends reveal a marriage of true love, steadfast despite dramatic adversities.

Dreams & Other True Tales   ISBN 978-1-58909-478-9
Someone asked me if I ever wrote fiction. "No," I said. "I have no need to dream up imaginary plots. I've too many bizarre stories from my own life: personal observations and experiences in Turkey, Poland, the U.S., Germany and China. Also included are other strange stories as told by my parents, a nephew in Izmir, cousins in Littlehampton and Berlin, a friend in former East Germany, my youngest brother and his daughter in Japan.
       Part I of the key story, "Dreams," is a saga of my maternal grandparents' (Eggert's and Anna's) hair-raising experiences emigrating separately from Germany in the mid-1880s, when they share dreams of meeting and marrying in Oregon. My mother recounted their oft-told adventures in interviews by the EW State Historical Society; her vivid recollections form the basis of Part I.